The Hamburger

The Ham

YALE UNIVERSITY PRESS   NEW HAVEN & LONDON

burger

A HISTORY

Josh Ozersky

A Caravan book. For more information, visit www.caravanbooks.org

Designed by Sonia Shannon
Set in Janson type by Integrated Publishing Solutions
Printed in the United States of America

Library of Congress Cataloging-in-Publication Data

Ozersky, Josh.
The hamburger : a history / Josh Ozersky.
p. cm.— (Icons of America series)
"A Caravan book"—T.p. verso.
Includes bibliographical references and index.
ISBN 978-0-300-11758-5 (clothbound)
1. Hamburgers—History. I. Title.
TX749.5.B43094 2008
641.8′4—dc22   2007043587

A catalogue record for this book is available from the British Library

10 9 8 7 6 5 4 3 2 1

Contents

The Hamburger

Sizzle and Symbolism

"Juicy, broiled hamburgers with just the right touch of charcoal taste from the fire have become an American institution." So states the stentorian narrator of *Beef Rings the Bell*, a promotional film produced in 1960 by the Union Pacific Railroad. The UP had good reason to want to promote beef, but the tone of the film is telling: there is no apology, no exposition, no tendentious defense of beef or beef eating. *Beef Rings the Bell* simply assumes that its audience loves beef, and the hamburger's primacy as the American beef meal par excellence is taken for granted.

"Even the process of broiling the hamburgers is fun, and promotes friendship and good fellowship." It's easy to laugh at the film's booming, hollow narration, which seems to embody every clichéd convention of Cold War propaganda, with its paternal pomposity and tossed-off nostrums about the American Way of

Life. And yet, it's true. Though today we would not put it so baldly, hamburger, *Beef Rings the Bell* understands, isn't just a sandwich; it is a social nexus. Even before the hamburger became a universal signifier of imperialism abroad and unwholesomeness at home, it had a special semiotic power—a quality not shared even by other great American sandwiches like the hot dog, the patty melt, the Dagwood, the Reuben, the po'boy, or even such totemic standards as fried chicken and apple pie. At the end of the day, nothing says America like a hamburger.

But just what is the content of this beefy, juicy, bun-bound message? What do Americans think of when they think of the hamburger? A robust, succulent spheroid of fresh ground beef, the birthright of red-blooded citizens? Or a Styrofoam-shrouded Big Mac, mass-produced to industrial specifications and served by wage slaves to an obese, brainwashed population? Is it a sizzling disc of goodness, served in a roadside restaurant dense with local lore, or the grim end product of a secret, sinister empire of tormented animals and unspeakable slaughtering practices? Is it cooking or commodity? An icon of freedom or the quintessence of conformity?

Like any other symbol, what the burger represents depends on who you ask. But the sandwich is not, like the flag or the vanished frontier, merely a plane upon which abstract national dreams are projected. The hamburger has its own history, a thick narrative line coming down through the chronicle of modern America. It's the story of European immigration in the nineteenth century and urbanization in the twentieth, as the German "Hamburg steak" evolved into hamburgers, gobbled by a rising class of urban factory workers. The sandwich later stars in the high-powered story of business on the march, as the hamburger, thanks to the innovations of the White Castle System and the McDonald's Corporation, became the Model T of prepared foods. It rides America's express lane to change via the postwar period's expanded highway system, inseparable from the suburban infrastructure that sprung up around it. And more: it closed up vast grasslands and built immense economies. It helped create the corporate culture that drives so many aspects of contemporary America. These realities made the burger matter and caused it to enter a plane of discourse where sandwiches rarely appear.

The hamburger was by midcentury already larger than gastronomy; its proper context was politics. As the hamburger became, in the form of McDonald's drive-ins, a medium of, as *Time* magazine called it in November 1961, "low-priced assembly-line feeding," it was noticed as a phenomenon of postwar America. Some people, then as now, saw in hamburgers merely cheapness and conformity, a kind of edible Levittown; on the other side was the kind of big business Babbittry represented by Ray Kroc and his fellow burger boosters.

In the decades that followed, what had been a rather mandarin revulsion among egghead circles would be taken up conversationally by a vastly expanded educated class of baby boomers. Fast food represented everything bad about America—its soullessness, its conformity, its vulgarity. As early as the 1960s, the high summer of the postwar boom, the perspective of ideologically marginal critics like Paul Goodman and C. Wright Mills began to pick up currency. By the 1970s, in the wake of Vietnam and Watergate, America's hamburger habit, to a lot of people, seemed merely laughable, a piece of Americana to be taken for granted. "The Communists are not about to take over our McDonald hamburger stands," Vietnam veteran John Kerry told the Senate Foreign Relations Committee in 1971, to appreciative laughter.

But the economic and cultural realities of America changed in the 1980s, and they are changing still. And with each change, the hamburger's place in our culture tacks and veers, blown by the winds of the zeitgeist. From the raw meat gnawed by Tatars to the boundless ambitions of Ray Kroc to the weed-dream of Harold and Kumar to the goosed-up versions, composed of foie gras and Kobe beef, that made headlines in the American Century's fin de siècle, the hamburger has reflected (and sometimes shaped) American life.

The hamburger, that is to say, isn't just an icon, a vehicle for "myth and symbol" musings by woolgathering academics. Studying its story is one way of studying the country that invented it, and then reinvented it again and again. The symbol is just the sizzle; the meat of the hamburger's meaning lies in how it changed the world, and why.

4

The Hamburg-American Line

First, let's get one thing straight. The hamburger is an American invention. It doesn't matter that it is named after a German city. It doesn't matter if Mongols used to ride around with minced horsemeat under their saddles, on their way to some hamburger-fueled havoc in the thirteenth century. These and other historical factlets figure prominently in most informal histories of the hamburger, both in print and on the Web. But the hamburger matters precisely because it is a universally understood food, a compact icon that has resisted all centrifugal pressure as it has moved around the world. Everywhere you go, a hamburger means a ground beef patty served on a white enriched bun. Occasionally, middlebrows replace the bun with a kaiser roll or some other unorthodox support. Here and there minor variations like the Oklahoman onion burger or the Mississippian slugburger appear and attain a local prominence. But the hamburger has resisted absorption nearly everywhere it goes, and a hundred years after its invention, it remains essentially the same object. Once that ground patty of browned beef was laid on a bun for the first time, the hamburger shimmered into existence philosophically. Because the burger has a kind of inevitability to it; it is a gastronomic endpoint, like sashimi or a baked potato. Its basic design cannot be improved upon.

It was a long time coming. The earliest reference to a proto-hamburger ancestor comes in 1763, in that year's edition of Hannah Glasse's *Art of Cookery, Made Plain and Easy*. This English cookbook describes a Hamburg sausage: "Take a pound of Beef, mince it very small, with half a Pound of the best Suet; then mix three Quarters of a Pound of Suet cut in large Pieces; then season it with Pepper, Cloves, Nutmeg, a great Quantity of Garlic cut small, some white Wine Vinegar, some Bay Salt, a Glass of red Wine, and one of Rum; mix all these very well together, then take the largest Gut you can find, stuff it very tight; then hang it up a Chimney, and smoke it with Saw-dust for a Week or ten Days; hang them in the Air, till they are dry, and they will keep a Year. They are very good boiled in Peas Porridge, and roasted with toasted Bread under it, or in an Amlet."[1]

They may have been good in an amlet, but they obviously were not hamburgers. Glasse's recipe is the *Australopithecus* of the hamburger family, a barely recognizable progenitor, primitive and inauspicious, but the missing link nonetheless —the earliest shared ancestor. And mark that last line: a sausage is far in spirit from a burger, and a beef sausage, roasted and served on toasted bread—that is something else again.

Hannah Glasse's afterthought, however, was a rare glimpse into the future: the nineteenth century would be an era of Hamburg steaks, minced or scraped beefsteaks, usually taken from a tough economy cut like the round and jazzed up with onions and a little nutmeg. Some recipes call for an egg as a binder; others, thriftier, add in some form of starchy filler. A reliable home meat grinder wasn't commonly available until the middle of the nineteenth century, so the home cooks of the period turned out something much closer to what we might call cube steak than a modern meat loaf, with its fine grain.[2] Like meat loaf, though, these were meant to be served with gravy. Most cookbooks of the nineteenth century contain some variation; by the time of Fannie Farmer's definitive *Boston Cooking-School Cook Book* (1896), the recipe was considered so common that it hardly required elaboration. "Shape, cook, and serve as meat cakes," the Martha Stewart of her time says laconically.[3] Hamburg steak was old hat, even by then—déclassé, a staple item.

Given the dish's provenance, it's not surprising. In Hamburg, particularly in the nineteenth century (and even to some extent today) beef was commonly served minced or chopped, a dish supposedly picked up from the Russians (Tatars).[4] Hamburg was an important port city and one of the major embarkation points for emigrants headed for the United States. Often these migrants were German. Hamburg steak was for them as familiar as Texas chili or Boston clam chowder, and about as prestigious. Cheap and nourishing and cooked up in a gratifying bath of butter, Hamburg steak was exactly the kind of street food you might expect to find in a port city where bustling people eat standing up. New York City was, even in colonial times, famously busy, and although restaurants per se were few, an ad hoc array of oyster stands, cookshops, coffeehouses, and freestanding food vendors accommodated local tastes. When the first real restaurants appeared, it was inevitable that hamburger steak would be present. Everyone liked it, for one thing; for another, it allowed for a big retail markup. Delmonico's, whose first printed menu appeared in 1837, lists the hamburger steak as its most expensive item at ten cents, twice the price of roast beef, pork chops, or a veal cutlet. Ten cents for a hamburger steak? The gravy train was rolling even then.

Interestingly, the chopped or minced or scraped Hamburg steak was itself a dressed-up version of a dish even lower on the culinary scale: salt beef. This makes sense on several levels. In the nineteenth century, fresh meat was a rarity in any city; this was the golden age of jerky, and an adulterated product like Hamburg steak is an obvious answer to the age-old dilemma of perishable meat. The recipe's English origin makes sense, too: obviously, people from Hamburg wouldn't call their own brand of minced beefsteak Hamburg steak any more than a coffee shop in Dallas serves Texas chili. Culinary historians like Theodora Fitz-Gibbon, in her *Food of the Western World*, are therefore wrong, in assuming that the dish comes from Germany via the Hamburg-American Line. That route didn't start until 1847, and anyway, the waves of German immigrants who flooded to America in the 1850s, refugees from political turmoil, arrived in America to find Hamburg steak ready to greet them.

What was a Hamburg steak like, through its long prehistory? It's clear from almost all extant nineteenth-century recipes that the gnarly, semicured beef patty clutched in the fingers of starving immigrants soon gave way to something resembling what we would think of today as Salisbury steak—the familiar, deliciously inorganic Swanson frozen dinner, with the brown greasy gravy and a few grim, gray onions on top. The dish was popular: it shows up in nearly every cookbook from Mary Lincoln's *Boston Cooking School Cook Book* in 1844 onward. But Hamburg steak never ascended to the level of the hot dog, a staple item whose Germanic origin was soon forgotten. It never became "steak" or even "meat loaf"; it remained "Hamburg steak" until it retreated forever into tinfoil trays and a few fugitive, dismal Pennsylvania roadhouses.

Why not? Part of it can surely be ascribed to bad luck. Many foods have aspired to iconic status, and one cannot help but project a rueful, thwarted mood to such once-beloved standards as roast ox, suckling pig, fish sticks, oyster pan roasts, and the rest.

They started out so well. Everyone loved them, and yet they made hardly any impression on the twentieth century. If you could figure out why not, you might have a better bead on the fault lines between their time and ours. For example, it's obvious that in the case of roast oxen, suckling pigs, venison haunches, and to some extent even roast turkey, these animals were just too big to cook in an ordinary household kitchen. Either they were relics of a rural age and couldn't fit in an oven, or (in the case of turkey) were simply too big to feed an average urban family and so were relegated to ceremonial appearances, like a retired comedy star who comes out once a year to accept a lifetime achievement award. People in the twentieth century more and more tended to live in cities rather than in the country, as the 1920 census announced. It's hard to manage an ox or a litter of squealing pigs in a modern city.

Talk of pigs brings up a larger question. If one were taking bets, circa 1850, as to what would eventually become the iconic American food, only a Nostradamus could have predicted that it would be made of beef. Pork was the American meat par excellence, and it was consumed on such a scale, and with such voracious appetite, that visitors frequently commented on it: pork was the perfect American commodity meat in every way. Pigs, like the people who owned them, were independent and self-willed, and more or less took care of themselves, eating whatever happened to be around. Pigs are cheap to keep, and a good investment, too: in a time before effective overland transportation, it cost too much to market corn, which weighs a lot in proportion to its value. But turn that corn into whiskey or pork, and now you have something that can bring cash into even the most remote economy. And most Americans lived in remote economies. Nor did this change if you lived in New York City right next door to Andrew Hamilton: cattle were a major investment, and you needed a lot of room and a lot of money to make them pay. (Cattle and capitalism are, not coincidentally, drawn from the same linguistic root, generative wealth being measured in herds for most of human history.) The economics of meat by the nineteenth century had long ago left sustenance farming far behind. The meat packers of Ohio, by midcentury, had "originated and perfected the system which packs 15 bushels of corn into a pig and packs that pig into a barrel, and sends him over the mountains and over the ocean to feed mankind."[5]

Moreover, as anyone who ever ate beef jerky will attest, pork is infinitely superior to beef as a preserved meat. Bacon, sausage, ham, salt pork—these were the staple items, and in some cases, the only nourishment, of generations of rural Americans, enslaved and free. Pork, writes Richard Osborn Cummings, in *The American and His Food: A History of Food Habits in the United States* (1940), "actually improves as a result of preservative processes. . . . It is said that because of its flavor value, a pound of bacon goes as far as three pounds of beef-steak."[6]

What changed in America was the opening of the Great Plains and the development of a massive meatpacking industry to accommodate cattle. This is one area of American life in which capitalism and the myth of the frontier cohere. In the early Republic, the plains had been considered a dead zone, the Great American Desert. But those sparse grasslands were just right for feeding vast herds of cattle. Nobody needs to be told about the resulting moment in American history; our heroes have always been cowboys. "Ten years and I'll have the Red River D on more cattle than you've looked at anywhere," John Wayne says, squinting into the future in Howard Hawks's *Red River* (1948). "I'll have that brand on enough beef to feed the whole country. Good beef for hungry people. Beef to make 'em strong, make 'em grow."

Though heavily mythologized, this wasn't too far from the truth. And Wayne's Tom Dunson is accurate in another way, too: he was in it for the money. Cowboys tamed the West, and cowboys were wage-earning functionaries employed by well-capitalized industrialists whose stated goal was to build mercantile empires. The inexorable western movement known as Manifest Destiny had as its object the acquisition of territory for Americans to live on, but the most active players in that movement were real estate speculators and others with commercial goals in mind, Babbitts rather than Bumpos. By the late nineteenth century, the opening of the vast, oceanic grasslands of the Great Plains to cattle ranching had made it possible for every American to enjoy beef more or less every day. In the 1880s dawned the Golden Age of Beef, when Gustavus Swift developed an infrastructure that linked Chicago's vast meatropolis with the

East Coast via refrigerated railroad cars.[7] For the first time these arterial lines carried fresh beef to cities overflowing with immigrant populations. Immigrants who liked to stretch a dollar, and make even newly cheap beef go a little bit farther. Immigrants who ate and bought a lot of Hamburg steak.

It was in cities, among the lower classes, that the Hamburg steak found its path to primacy. Pigs may have been okay for settlers in the rude woods. But modern America was to be urban, industrial, and capitalistic. It had workers to feed, and they wanted cheap and nourishing beef lunches. More important, it had a "beef trust" in place by the 1880s that controlled the burgeoning traffic from the Midwest to the cities of the East. The "beef trust" would come in for much public criticism early in the next century, when Upton Sinclair published *The Jungle*; but in the years of industrialization, the availability of beef to even the poorest workers was a feat of which many Americans were justly proud.

There was, and is, no symbol of bounty to compare to fresh beef. Americans followed their British forebears in regarding it as a peerless sign of health and prosperity.[8] There was no question about its supremacy. "Instinctively most persons prefer beef, as an habitual article of diet, to any other variety of meat," wrote Dr. Austin Flint confidently in 1866's *Physiology of Man*.[9] And the fact that America boasted so much of it was always an article of patriotic pride, long before beef was available to even the poorest city dwellers. Americans ate beef as a birthright. "Our chief article of food was beef," boasted Richard Henry Dana earlier in the century in *Two Years before the Mast* (1840). "What one man ate over a hearty man's allowance would have made an English peasant's heart leap in his mouth."[10]

Hamburg steak was the cheapest way for the poorest Americans to eat beef. It was the rock-bottom entry point to the American beef dream. And as such, it contains the essence of the hamburger story. Hamburgers don't taste better than beefsteaks, nor are they more native to these shores than a hundred other favorite dishes, from burgoo to barbecue. They are popular because they are made of the substance all people love most, if Dr. Flint is to be believed, and available everywhere in more or less the same form for very little cash. There is an inevitability to the hamburger: it is the most concentrated way a person can cheaply eat everything that people like about beef. As food historian Elisabeth Rozin has written with lyrical precision, "The meaning of the burger is as a kind of common denominator of the beef experience, with all the flavor, aroma, tenderness, and juiciness in a cheap and accessible form. The meatiness, the beefiness, the succulence of the fat are all there in that unassuming patty. For perhaps the first time ever, the hunger for all that beef represents, [could] easily be satisfied, available to almost anyone."[11]

But not yet. The hamburger dream was still mired in the chaos of the nineteenth century. Here was an immigrant dish whose origin nobody was sure of, whose preparation varied from cook to cook, that was unwieldy to eat and complicated to prepare, with its elaborate requirements of grinding or scraping or mincing and folding in minced onions, that required a greasy pan gravy, and a fork and knife to eat, not to mention a plate, which then required a table and chair, and, like its closest living descendant, meat loaf, had to be served cooked all the way through.

None of that mattered, of course, if you were making it at home. But dishes don't become iconic by being served at the dinner table. Totems exist in the public space. And until the Hamburg steak could be standardized, commercialized, and exploited for profit by Americans everywhere, it would never become the universal American food. It would eventually get its Edisons and Fords, but the path this strange "meat cake" took through what historian Robert Wiebe has called America's "search for order" remains a strange one.[12] That it finally arrived, on a bun and called by its proper name, by the early twentieth century, is certain. But what a long and twisted route it took!

This being a history of the hamburger, it's necessary to try to sort out who made the first one. There are a number of rival claims, but they're all equally worthless, historically speaking. None can produce any real evidence. Still, none seem to be made of whole cloth, and the earliest claim, of 1885, is recent enough not to strain credulity. It comes on behalf of a Seymour, Wisconsin, teenager named Charlie Nagreen who may or may not have put a meatball between two slices of bread and sold it as a sandwich from his ox-drawn cart at the Outagamie County Fair that year.

Decades later, "Hamburger Charlie" was a fixture at the fair and had sold hamburgers as long as anybody could remember. The claim seemed viable enough by 1990 that Seymour built the Hamburger Hall of Fame and soon took to throwing an elaborate "Burgerfest" every year, culminating in the creation, in 2001, of an eight-thousand-pound burger. This was a fitting tribute to a man who loved hamburgers enough to have claimed to invented them and who may well have invented them, as far as he knew.

Another claim comes via the city of Hamburg, New York. Two Ohio brothers, Frank and Charles Menches, are said to have sold a ground beef sandwich at the Erie County Fair in Hamburg in 1885. It is this coincidence that gives a whiff of fraud to the Menches claim, which is taken almost as seriously in Ohio and Hamburg as Nagreen's is in Seymour. The transition from Hamburg steak to hamburgers is an obvious one that required no serendipitous inventions in the town of Hamburg. (Charles Menches supposedly made the burger that fateful day because he didn't have any pork, and then he named it after the town.) To make this claim even weaker, the hamburger the Menches made wasn't a hamburger at all but some kind of debased meat loaf— it features brown sugar, coffee, and "other spices." On top of everything else, the Menches also claim to have invented the ice cream cone.

The most commonly recognized of the undocumented early claims seems to be that of Fletcher Davis, an Athens, Texas, vendor whose hamburger sandwiches are said to have been the hit of the 1904 Saint Louis World's Fair. Most hamburger history research begins and ends with a Google search and invariably leads to a book by the late Frank X. Tolbert, a former columnist for the Dallas *Morning News*. "It took me years of sweatneck research," Tolbert wrote, "before I finally determined" that Davis, like Tolbert a native of Henderson County, "invented the hamburger sandwich." Tolbert's account of how "Old Dave" sold a sandwich at the fair's midway has been accepted by so many food historians that 2004 was widely celebrated as the hamburger's centennial. The key event in this version, akin to Lana Turner being discovered at Schwab's Drug Store, is a New York *Tribune* article that hails "a new sandwich called a hamburger, 'the innovation of a food vendor on the pike.'" The *Tribune* article, which does not exist, has been quoted everywhere; its real source seems to be Tolbert himself.[13]

Louis' Lunch restaurant, in New Haven, Connecticut, on the other hand, has a claim that is both earlier and better documented in its favor. A venerable institution, it has operated continuously since 1895, and a nosegay of affidavits attest that the place has been making hamburgers since the turn of the century. (These affidavits are not irrefutable either, but at least they exist.) The same family operates it today, using the same vertical broilers as did the restaurant's founder, Louis Lassen. The experience of eating there is an elevating one. There are so many names and symbols carved into the wood counter that it resembles a Jackson Pollock painting. The place is saturated likewise with the minute, unmistakable marks of its history, which hangs heavy over every meal. The ancient vertical broilers, tall and narrow, are made of heavy black cast iron, ornately carved in the beaux arts style. A deep blue flame burns inside them, high and luminous. Signs everywhere announce a long-standing prohibition against ketchup and mustard. There is just one problem. The next hamburger Louis' Lunch serves will be its first. Like Charlie Nagreen, Fletch Davis, the Menches Brothers, and everyone who ever got hungry when there was chopped meat in the house, Louis serves a ground beef sandwich on sliced bread, in this case toast. And that is not a hamburger.

A hamburger—unlike a Hamburg steak sandwich, a meatball sandwich, a meatloaf sandwich, a patty melt, the German *Frikadelle*, or a thousand other conceivable variations—is defined by its being served on a bun. Given how much juice even a small hamburger produces, thin slices of bread will soak through quickly, and thick slices will get in the way, sticking to the roof of your mouth and absorbing all the flavor. Toast, as at Louis', is a stopgap measure that no one ever bothered to imitate. No, there is no doubt: on any kind of semantic or platonic level, no bun = no burger. There has always been ground meat, and there have always been sandwiches, the earl and his publicity machine notwithstanding. But almost its entire existence, a hamburger has meant ground beef served on a bun. To admit ground beef on toast as a hamburger is to make the idea of a "hamburger" so loose, so abstract, so semiotically promiscuous as to have no meaning.

And we know that it does have meaning. Hamburgers exist in the public consciousness of Americans; in fact, the case could be made that one of the things that defines us as Americans is our ability to recognize a hamburger as a bundle of meaning, not just a bundle of meat. A picture of a hamburger should be on the citizenship test; it's much more relevant to American life than George Washington is. (One proof of this is that no one exchanges a picture of a hamburger for a George Washington.) The historical record is full of meat sandwiches that didn't mean anything to people beyond a quick meal. The *Los Angeles Times*, for example, in 1894 mentions a late-night short-order stand that sold tamales to drunks—along with "trotters, ham, [and] egg and hamburger steak sandwiches."[14]

The only assertion to have first made a hamburger on a bun, out of all the clamor and claims, belongs to the Bilby family of Tulsa, Oklahoma. Their drive-in restaurant, Weber's, was founded in 1933 and is probably better known for its root beer than for its hamburgers. Weber's claims that its family patriarch, Oscar Bilby, had been serving hamburgers on buns at huge picnics on the family farm for over forty years before the restaurant's founding: "On the fourth of July, 1891, Oscar probably made his most significant contribution to society when he forged a piece of iron into a 3′ × 4′ grill. He then built a pit and heated the grill with hickory wood. His wife, Fanny, made sour dough buns while Oscar pattied up some black angus all-beef-patties and proceeded to grill the patties on his new hand-made grill."[15]

The grill, still in use, has Oscar's initials and the year of its forging carved in, like an imperial dynasty's sacred sword. The story is impossible to verify, but that didn't stop popular Oklahoma historian Michael Wallis from broadcasting it or Oklahoma governor Frank Keating from proclaiming it. (Similar ceremonial statements, invariably accompanied by an oversized document festooned with official seals, have been produced by officials in Connecticut, New York, and Wisconsin.) The Tulsa claim is the pearl of the burger apocrypha and stands for having never been challenged. But it's still less than solid. Bilby's burger, however perfect it may have been, happened in the vacuum of obscurity, a tree falling in the forest if there ever was one.

And it's doubtful, besides, if any private hamburger can be said to be historically significant, even had Matthew Brady been present to photograph it coming off the grill. The hamburger—compact, standardized, and mass-produced, coming at the world as an irrepressible economic and cultural force—matters because of the infrastructure created for it and how it changed the world. The hamburger, wave rather than particle, is a public commercial entity. But it adds some credence to the Bilby family's claim that, as it happens, the first great modern hamburger, on a bun and ready for business, was conceived just a few hundred miles to the north of Tulsa, in nearby Wichita, Kansas. It is there, under the care of a fry cook named Walter Anderson, that the true story of the hamburger begins.

"All This from a Five-Cent Hamburger!"

In 1926, Edgar Waldo "Billy" Ingram, the Henry Ford of hamburgers, effused in his company newsletter that "when the word 'hamburger' is mentioned one immediately thinks of the circus, or carnival, or the county fairs, or even of the dirty, dingy, ill-lighted hole-in-the-wall, down in the lower districts of the city. The day of the dirty, greasy hamburger is past. No more shall we be privileged to taste the hamburger at the circuses and carnivals only, for a new system has arisen, the 'White Castle System.'"[1]

The *Hot Hamburger* newsletter, in which this prophetic statement can be found, would later be renamed the *White Castle House Organ* and printed on glossy stock. But the original, residing in the Ohio Historical Society, is little more than a mimeographed sheet of typewritten onionskin. It looks like a junior-high book report, such as a well-meaning but mistake-prone

```
                HOT  HAMBURGER

                "Just off the griddle."
```

Vol. 1.	January 1, 1926,	No. 3.

THE HAMBURGER AS A STABILIZED FOOD PRODUCT.

When the word "hamburger" is mentioned one immediately thinks of the circus, or carnival, or the county fairs, or even of the dirty, dingy, ill-lighted hole-in-the-wall, down in the lower districts of the city.

The day of the dirty, greasy hamburger is past. No more shall we be privileged to taste the hamburger at the circuses and carnivals only, for a new system has arisen, the "White Castle System."

The hamburger contains the three main items of the American diet, Namely bread, meat and vegetables, properly proportioned in exact amounts to make a nutricious sandwich.

A revelation in the eating business has come. Instead of having to go to a restaurant and wait half an hour for the noon lunch, one may step into a nearby hamburger establishment and partake of the hot, juicy hamburger, prepared instantaneously.

They may be taken out in parcels to the homes, on pleasure trips, picnics, etc. and as a well known St. Louis magazine puts it, "the sandwiches are not alone as cheap as they were ever served but a better and more palatable sandwich than was served several years ago.

The materials used are selected and purchased from establishments who specialize in their particular line, and are served by men who have served their apprenticeship in the hamburger business.

Through constant study and application of all concerned the lowly hamburger is gradually winning it's way and has become one of the most economical foods available to the public.

"A new system has arisen": the dawn of White Castle announced in its first newsletter.

student might turn in. White Castle, meanwhile, was at the time a regional chain selling nickel hamburgers in a few midsized wheat-belt cities.

And yet the note of triumphalism is unmistakable. (Who would think of bragging about the "privilege" of eating hamburgers?) The full flowering of commercial culture in the 1920s, an aftershock of the Great War's privations and Puritanism, gives the decade its tonic note; and it is this key, an ebullient, radiant, unsprung crassness, that sings to us in missives like one above. On one hand, Ingram was right in everything he wrote: the company he cofounded did change the way people ate hamburgers, and the change was not just a minor dietary one. Ingram could not have known that the hamburger would eventually become a multibillion-dollar business that would extend American culture from China to Peru, but he spoke of his little chain of burger stands in tones reserved to world conquerors, and that spirit is in no small part responsible for White Castle's success.

It was very much the spirit of business in the 1920s. It wasn't just rhetoric; this was the age of big dreams and expansive plans, when positive thinking and big money seemed within the reach of any entrepreneur with the spirit to strike it big. It was the hour of the Ponzi scheme, the years of Dr. Émile Coué and his mantra of "Every day, in every way, I am getting better and better." As has been the case from time to time in American cultural history, God and Mammon were as one in that acquisitive era, and making money seemed divinely sanctified to those Protestant businessmen who barreled the nation into modernity. "The man who builds a factory builds a temple," President Calvin Coolidge had said a few years earlier. "The man who works there worships there." The ultimate expression of messianic Babbittry came from Bruce Barton, the advertising magnate who popularized Coolidge's remarks in his immortal *The Man Nobody Knows* (1925), an account of Jesus Christ, "the founder of modern business."[2]

For Barton, Jesus was the ultimate salesman, a true believer who knew how to get his message across: "What, then were the principle elements in his power over men? How was it is that the boy from a country village became the greatest leader? First of all he had the voice and manner of the leader—the personal magnetism which begets loyalty and commands respect. . . . [But] the essential element in personal magnetism is a consuming sincerity—an overwhelming faith in the importance of the work one has to do."[3]

Jesus was above all else, for Barton, "an adman: persuading, recruiting followers, finding the right words to arouse interest and create desires, in short exemplifying all the principles of modern salesmanship." We find in *The Man Nobody Knows* a comic artifact today, possibly one bordering on blasphemy; but it does an injustice to the 1920s zeitgeist to think of Barton as a crank. It is no accident that he helped found BBDO, a global agency synonymous with modern advertising. For Barton, there was no dishonesty involved. Advertising was his vocation, and he took it seriously, even sanctimoniously. This is America at its most righteously materialistic; the critical literary culture, from H. L. Mencken to the modernists abroad in Paris, made no impression on it at all. Everyone was on board for the big win, and as a number of cultural historians have eloquently pointed out, advertising was in many ways the spiritual life of the new era. "It is great power that has been entrusted to your keeping," Coolidge told an audience of advertisers in 1926, "which charges you with the high responsibility of inspiring and ennobling the commercial world. It is all part of the greater work of the regeneration and redemption of mankind."[4]

White Castle, from the first, was built on full-throated propaganda. It is as inseparable from its success as beef and bun. Its product, a thin hamburger served on an enriched white bun, and the dedicated restaurant that served as the hamburger's delivery system were undoubtedly innovations that belong in the Smithsonian alongside the *Spirit of St. Louis;* but without Ingram's genius for marketing, they would have been anonymous and inert— just another good sandwich, at most nostalgia for Wichita-area oldsters. Neither, though, can Billy Ingram be said to be the sole author of White Castle. At its heart was a technological innovation utterly in keeping with modern times. White Castle's success in the 1920s expresses the most dynamic trends that swirled around the period and that, once unloosed, helped to generate the world we live in today. Something that had been vital but diffused, the hamburger, was perfected as a mechanized, rationalized, Taylorized technique; modern messaging gave it its identity; and a vast centralized bureaucracy came into being to administer it as a corporation. White Castle was born, flowered, expanded, and eventually withered, to be replaced by a far more successful entity that would go on to conquer the world. But in the beginning, it was the idea of two men.

White Castle began in 1916 in Wichita, the artistic brainstorm of a fry cook named Walter Anderson. Anderson, he would later explain, had worked in a local restaurant, cooking the kind of ad hoc, ill formed, vaguely spheroid burgers typical of the time. Anderson ate burgers on his own time and was a tireless experimenter. History has not recorded whether he invented the modern hamburger all at once, but he deserves the credit for first thinking to:

- cook the burger on a very hot (500°F) dedicated grill, so that it would be deliciously brown on the outside and still relatively juicy inside;
- press the burger with the back of his spatula, flattening it down and out and reducing all its flavor to one plane;
- replace sliced bread with a specially designed white bun; and
- put onions next to the burger on the grill to bathe in the juices from the still-cooking meat.

These combined advances were the building blocks of the modern hamburger. To the end of his days, Billy Ingram was fond of showing the custom spatula he had developed for the White Castle Company from saw-blade steel, for extra strength in mashing down hamburgers. (The spatula now resides, as appropriate for a holy relic, in the Ohio State Historical Society, stored in a temperature-proof glass case.) The spatula is, in fact, an utterly apt symbol for White Castle's advance. The flattened, disc-shaped hamburgers would all look the same, and even a small one could cover enough surface area to justify a sandwich of its own. Its seared surface would register on the palate as a contrast with the bread above it and the juice beneath it; you could even play the contrast up further by adding soft condiments like sautéed onions, ketchup, or mustard. Surface area is everything in the modern hamburger, but it's literally true of the White Castle, as it would late come to be known. As "castle operators" came to stretch their beef more and more aggressively, the burger, which must have been something close to a typical

E. W. "Billy" Ingram shows the spatula that started it all.

midcentury five-and-dime hamburger, became a sliver of meat, often less than an ounce before cooking. At this point, the White Castle became a confection, a kind of beef petit four, and nonetheless delicious for that.

White Castle would be limited, in the years to come, by the extremity of its minimalist aesthetic. Even people who like thin hamburgers want some substance, and at least a little bit of resistance, when they bite down. But in establishing a morphological paradigm, Walt Anderson opened the door for every other classically constructed hamburger. These would imitate his cooking innovation, just as their businesses would mimic White Castle's seminal ability to replicate itself across the country, via Kremlin-like management, a ready-to-go infrastructure, and a brand that beamed like a watch house in the night. All these helped White Castle succeed on a grand scale, spreading flat little hamburgers across the country like a virus, with each burger carrying the essential information for the construction of a mutant chain, different (barely) only in name: White Tower, White Rose, White Clock, White Palace, and even Royal Castle.

But this all came later and drew on something even more fundamental than the system or the slider. The key to Anderson's masterpiece was the bun. It was the bun that gave the hamburger its mobility; that allowed a person to eat it while walking or (more important) while driving; it was the bun that made it special, that separated it from all other sandwiches and gave it a brandable identity. The essence of a picture is the frame, as G. K. Chesterton once observed, and so the essence of the hamburger is the bun. No less an authority than Ronald L. McDonald, a scion of the McDonald's founding clan, wrote in his magisterial *The Complete Hamburger:* "[Anderson] did something no one else had ever done—he developed a bun specifically for the hamburger sandwich. The dough he selected was heavier than ordinary bread dough, and he formed it into small, square shapes that were just big enough for one of his new flat hamburgers. The bun was then baked to a golden brown, giving it a denser crust on the top and bottom so the juices wouldn't soak through so quickly."[5]

As McDonald well understood, the bun didn't just hold the burger, it was inextricably a part of the whole, and when perfectly constructed, as at White Castle, the patty's perimeter was flush with its own. A hamburger is no mere sandwich, thrown together at home for convenient eating at the gaming table or the TV room, a random pile of starch and meat. No, it is a product of modern industrial manufacturing, each burger as artfully self-contained as a Homeric hexameter. The bun and the burger were created for each other and spoke of their symbiosis in the language of circumferential geometry.

Anderson opened his hamburger stand in 1916, on November 16, with a flat metal griddle, a counter, three stools, and a spatula. He had to get his beef and buns on credit, paying back a local grocer out of the morning's proceeds: $3.75. Even bad hamburger stands made money, but Anderson's was the best, and he soon opened another, and then a third. Hamburgers, though, were a marginal business, a trash food for workers; you couldn't get a bank loan to expand a business selling hamburgers. It would be like trying to get a bank loan today for a falafel wagon. Moreover, Anderson had a credit rating that, he later said, "would horrify either Dunn or Bradstreet" and a financial statement that "would chase a film of glass across the eyes of the softest-hearted banker in the city."[6] The product and the entrepreneur were both suspect in the eyes of the town's burghers, who still thought of hamburger stands as "dirty, dingy, ill-lighted hole-in-the-wall, down in the lower districts of the city." The site of the fourth stand was owned by a respectable dentist who expressed reservations about the business. But luckily for Anderson, his real estate broker, who, as it happened, had in fact worked for Dunn and Bradstreet, saw what he was trying to do and was not horrified at all. In fact, he was intrigued. A faraway twinkle appeared in the realtor's eye, and he guaranteed the loan himself. Then he asked Anderson if he wanted a partner. The realtor's name was Edgar Waldo "Billy" Ingram.

Ingram was the genius who invented White Castle as a business and who created the template for all fast-food restaurants in the world. He wasn't an executive on the order of Ray Kroc, and his "system" was nowhere near as sleek as the McDonald brothers' would be. But at the art of marketing he was unsurpassed. Ingram was the archetype of the 1920s booster, a boundlessly optimistic businessman with horizons untroubled by modernist doubts. A true avatar of the Coolidge Prosperity, he poured himself into promoting and perfecting the White Castle System. "A revelation in the eating business has come. Instead of having to go to a restaurant and waste half an hour of the noon lunch, one may step into a nearby hamburger establishment and partake of the hot, juicy hamburger, prepared instantaneously."

This panegyric, taken from *Hot Hamburger*, was for employees only. Ingram's boosting where the public was concerned was such as Barton might have imputed to Our Lord. In 1930 he arranged for the physiological chemistry department of the University of Minnesota to perform a scientific experiment. A medical student would be kept on a strict diet of White Castle hamburgers and water for thirteen weeks. The student, Ingram would later report triumphantly, "maintained good health for the entire three months and was eating 20 to 24 hamburgers a day during the last few weeks."[7] According to Ingram, an unnamed "food scientist" even "signed a report that a normal healthy child could eat nothing but our hamburger and water, and fully develop all its physical and mental faculties."[8]

One child? A generation! One of the great things about Ingram's message was the complete absence in it of any hint of limitation in the virtues of the White Castle hamburger. It was the ideal food for all people at all times. In the 1930s the expanding chain began to encounter resistance from middle-class women, who had somehow got the notion that hamburgers were a less than ideal choice for families and entertaining. Ingram set out to conquer the notion by creating an iconic White Castle "hostess" after the model of Betty Crocker. Julia Joyce, portrayed by a forceful, prim lady named Ella Louise Agniel, was deputized to spread the word to her sisters everywhere. Her identity was a well-kept secret, and Julia spent the 1930s explaining how White Castle hamburgers were the perfect choice for tea parties and family dinners and reassuring skeptical matrons about the

---

Only U. S. Government
Inspected Beef

"Buy 'em
by the Sack"

LUNCHEONS AND SUPPERS
(*See also under "Hot Weather Suggestions"*)

Luncheons and Suppers
(*Continued*)

MENU No. 1
White Castle Hamburger Sandwiches
Creamed Mushrooms   Celery
Chocolate Mocha Layer Cake
Coffee

MENU No. 2
White Castle Hamburger Sandwiches
Tomato and Cucumber Salad
Caramel Custard   Coffee

MENU No. 3
White Castle Hamburger Sandwiches
Cream of Lima Beans
Health Salad
Oatmeal Cookies   Coffee

MENU No. 4
White Castle Hamburger Sandwiches
Hot Potato Salad   Stuffed Olives
Boston Cream Pie   Coffee

MENU No. 5
White Castle Hamburger Sandwiches
Cucumber-Pineapple Jelled Salad
Ripe Olives
Wafers   Coffee

MENU No. 6
White Castle Hamburger Sandwiches
Boston Baked Beans
Glazed Baked Apple   Coffee

MENU No. 7
White Castle Hamburger Sandwiches
Peas and Carrots in Cream
Saratoga Chips
Apricot Pie   Coffee

MENU No. 8
Tomato Juice Cocktail
White Castle Hamburger Sandwiches
Candied Sweet Potatoes
Prune Whip   Coffee

MENU No. 9
White Castle Hamburger Sandwiches
Scalloped New Cabbage
Currant Jelly   Relish
Sand Cookies   Coffee

MENU No. 10
White Castle Hamburger Sandwiches
Creamed String Beans
Green Onions and Celery
Cherry Tarts   Coffee

[8]

[9]

White Castle as tea sandwiches? Why not?

32

flawless hygiene and salutary atmosphere of White Castle restaurants.

This was an easy matter, since even a glance at a White Castle was designed to reassure people about its cleanliness. That, after all, was the whole genesis of the White Castle brand. (As a former realtor, Ingram presumably knew the value of curb appeal.) As he explained it, "The 'White' signifies purity and cleanliness, and 'Castle' represents strength, permanence, and stability."[9] In looking for a distinctive visual motif, Ingram turned to the epitome of Midwestern strength and permanence, the gothic lines of the Chicago Water Tower, one of the few structures to survive the city's Great Fire.

The visual language of White Castle said a number of things to its customers. First, and most quintessentially American, was the shameless, outsized hype of the thing. Here was a 250-square-foot stand selling nickel hamburgers, and it announced itself as a pinnacle of stately stability. Then there was the matter of its whiteness. Ingram's emphasis on cleanliness was far from misplaced: hamburgers, like sausages, were widely considered the final resting place of every kind of scrap and offal. That had been the unintended message of Upton Sinclair's novel *The Jungle* (1904), an exposé of the meatpacking business so revolting that the public outcry helped bring federal health regulation into being. (Sinclair had meant the book as a primer on worker exploitation; America just wanted more reliable meat.) Ingram never tired of inventing ways to reassure the public about the wholesomeness of White Castle beef, but the concept of cleanliness informed the creation of the physical restaurant. The very walls of White Castle bore a message.

It was more than the walls, though. They were the most obvious and memorable of the restaurant's physical features, but the messaging continued once you walked through the door. What Julia Joyce said about one White Castle held true everywhere, because *all the White Castles had to be the same.* Ingram understood before anyone else that he was building, not just a hamburger chain, but an identity, what today would be called a brand. Not only did it have to be good, it had to be unique, and somehow he had to find a way of keeping every new White Castle just like the original—even if it were hundreds of miles away and far beyond his control. If he could, by sheer bureaucratic force of will and the strength of his vision, convince the go-getters (poised with him for White Castle's Great Leap Forward) to hew the line, he would at long last have created a national hamburger. It was a worthy goal, a universal meal that would be completely American, unmarred by distinctions of region, class, or ethnicity. Out of many, one—just like the meat of a well-ground hamburger.

Ingram never let a chance go by to brag about White Castle's triumphant homogeneity. "When you sit in a White Castle," a 1932 brochure reminded customers, "remember that you are one of several thousands; you are sitting on the same kind of stool; you are being served on the same kind of counter; the coffee you drink is made in accordance with a certain formula; the hamburger you eat is prepared in exactly the same way over a gas flame of the same intensity; the cups you drink from are identical with thousands of cups that thousands of other people are using at the same moment; the same standard of cleanliness protects your food. . . . Even the men who serve you are guided by standards of precision which have been thought out from beginning to end."[10] O happy thought! Alas, it wasn't exactly so. Ingram, like Henry Ford, dreamed of an infinite and malleable labor force, one that could be counted on to run White Castles the right way. To help them on their way, the company produced minutely detailed instructions for operators on how to dress, how to speak, what to wear, and so on, down to the length of their fingernails. These instructions, which came with a photograph of an ideal White Castle counterman to measure oneself against, were supplemented by tips in *Hot Hamburger*, soon renamed prosaically as the *White Castle House Organ*.

Ingram was up against an insoluble problem with his labor force. On one hand, he dreamt, as Ford and other business barons had, of a docile and predictable labor force, "guided by standards of precision" set by senior management. But on the other hand, White Castle was an entrepreneurial-collectivist dream, a network of salesmen who together would march forward into the future under the White Castle banner. Something had to give. In White Castle's case, it was the entrepreneurial idea. White Castle's corporate activity in the 1920s centered on the drive for standardized, rationalized procedures. Operators were asked to fill out questionnaires in which they described their exact methods of cooking: how many hamburgers they got from a pound of meat, whether they were fried with suet or without, what the meat to fat mixture was, down to the formula of the bun. Naturally, given how spread-out White Castle was and the fact that the world had never yet experienced the creation of a truly universal hamburger methodology, these were maddeningly diverse. The company did all it could to counter this, even buying a slick maroon-and-gold Curtis OX-5 Travel Air biplane, which Billy Ingram himself flew around the country, making spot inspections.

And such rigor did not go unrewarded: as much as was possible (by 1930 White Castle had 116 restaurants spread over 1,424 miles), White Castle's restaurants set the standard for standardization. By 1927 a standard White Castle restaurant was an exquisite machine, dynamically engineered to allow one man to sell coffee and hamburgers, supremely efficient and gleaming with chrome and white enamel. Its frame was a prefabricated steel structure ("the most inviting and attractive design of commercial building anywhere," according to Ingram) built of 149 pieces of steel, with "every joint tightened to the last thread."[11] It was mobile, fire-resistant, and as self-contained as Skylab. All its paper products were made by a White Castle subsidiary. Soon enough its buns and burgers were too, as Ingram decisively replaced the fresh meat that was White Castle's reason for being with the preportioned frozen patties we know and dread today.

White Castle
SYSTEM, INC.

№ 631

SUGGESTION BLANK

City *CINCINNATI OHIO* Date *3 - 24 - 1946*

The White Castle System welcomes and will investigate any new or original idea, suggestion or criticism from members of its organization in relation to the Company and its personnel, the operation and

appearance of a Castle or equipment, or the improvement of its products or their sale. Awards will be made for all suggestions adopted according to the rules and instructions on the back of this sheet.

Use this space for presenting your suggestion. Be sure to state clearly what improvement or benefit, in your opinion, will result from its adoption.

O 1/4" HOLE

PATTIE OF MEAT
FROZEN

I HAVE DISCOVERED BY PUTTING THIS HOLE IN THE MEAT, IT WILL COOK FASTER IT ALSO ALLOWES THE STEAM TO COME UP THROUGH THE HOLE AND STILL RETAIN ALL OF ITS FLAVOR, I HAVE TIMED THIS PROSSESS OF COOKING THE MAMBURGERS AND I BELIVE IT IS A THIRD FASTER, IF THIS HOLE WAS PROSSESED IN IT WHILE BEING MANUFACTORED IT WOUL BE BETTER, OTHER WISE IT WOULD BE TO SLOW TO DO IT OUR SELVES, By THE HOLE IN THE MEAT IT DOES ALLOW IT TO COOK FASTER, THAT IS THE IDEA I AM TRYING TO EXPLAIN.

DO NOT SIGN YOUR NAME
Retain numbered duplicate for your information and identification

A White Castle operator's invention of burger holes, preserved for history at the Ohio Historical Society.

The romance of standardization is one of the hardest things to imagine, much less sympathize with. Taking mass production for granted, we tend to identify it with suburban sprawl, with monopoly and monotony, with armies of "cookie-cutter" houses and cars, soldiering endlessly onward like a legion of cold-eyed robots. But the high modern period was positively in love with standardization. It was a grail and a gift, the summit of up-to-the-minute living. For many intellectuals World War I had effectively ended the dream so eloquently described in the optimism of figures like George Bernard Shaw and H. G. Wells. But this tended to be a European phenomenon. The hero of Edward Bellamy's *Looking Backward* (1888), a phenomenally successful science fiction novel, simply sleeps through the bad parts of the twentieth century, the mustard gas and machine guns, and when he awakens in 2000, the world is run as a benevolent, mechanized superstate where everybody is happy. This, without too much exaggeration, was the mindset of the 1920s (minus the socialism). The Machine Age, as it was called, was a big hit with its beneficiaries. Henry Ford was a culture hero, and the invention of the assembly line hailed as a triumph that produced high wages and cheap cars.

But there was more to Fordism than the goods it produced. *People liked standardization for its own sake.* Part of this has to do with Robert Wiebe's "search for order," a central energy in the American zeitgeist during the chaotic years of development in the late nineteenth and early twentieth centuries.[12] But beyond that, Americans of the 1920s were intoxicated with consumer culture. Advertising came into its own in this period, along with credit cards, conspicuous consumption, a shift from rural to urban living, and all the other hallmarks of people who love to shop. This transformation didn't happen overnight, but it really arrived in the 1920s. In 1887 R. H. Macy had promised "goods suitable for the millionaire, at prices suitable for the millions."[13] The modern world had delivered that, and most of all in America, where consumption and patriotism inextricably commingled. To this day, sunshine patriots proclaim America's greatness owing to "our way of life," as if every other industrialized country didn't offer the same standard of living. But in the 1920s, the high summer of modernism, America really was the promised land of technology, the vanguard of creature comforts and streamlined dreams.

We have come so far from this point of view, particularly in regard to food, that Billy Ingram's evangelical zeal for uniformity strikes us as weird.

The thought of endless hamburgers, endlessly replicated across America, is more likely to seem like a nightmare today, like a virus or the invasion of the body snatchers. Food should be fresh, local, lovingly prepared; it should be the stuff of craft. To say that something is canned is the worst aspersion you can make. And yet, a historian of canning in 1924 could effuse, "Canning gives the American family . . . a kitchen where all good things grow, and where it is always harvest time, a regular Arabian nights garden where raspberries, apricots, olives, and pine-apples, always ripe, grow side by side with peas, pumpkins, spin-ach; a garden with baked beans, vines and spaghetti bushes, and sauerkraut beds, and great cauldrons of hot soup, and through it running a branch of the ocean in which one can catch salmon, lobsters, crabs and shrimp, and dig oysters and clams."[14]

Thus the burgers at White Castle were formed into perfect squares, perfectly regular, so that they could *fill up every square inch of the griddle*, without wasting an inch. This was the kind of Faustian mind that bought the machine age into being, and White Castle was one of its quintessential expressions. The essence of the new industrial philosophy was this: immense economies of scale rewarded big operations and (by extension) big thinkers. Even something so small as a hamburger could become a mighty engine of prosperity. When White Castle's building and paper divisions had become profitable businesses in their own right, churning out identical goods for gas stations and diners everywhere, factory visitors, according to Billy Ingram, would often marvel at his empire's lowly origin. "It is not unusual for visitors, after they have been through the Porcelain Steel and Paperlynen factories and the General Offices, to pause and exclaim, 'All this from a 5-cent Hamburger!'"[15]

"More and more as time goes on," Ingram confided to a meeting of like-minded businessmen in 1964, "I share their amazement."[16] The address, Ingram's valediction, was published, with exquisite ink drawings of scenes from the life of White Castle, under the name "'All This from a 5-Cent Hamburger': The Story of the White Castle System." Every American with a love of hamburgers should own one.

White Castle's success was easy to emulate; it was the very nature of the "system" that it required little in the way of individual genius to make it run. The reason hamburgers became the lingua franca of fast food, and subsequently the default National Food of America, lay in how easily other companies could and did shamelessly rip off White Castle. Even at its height, White Castle was a tiny chain by modern standards, but to paraphrase the old saying about the Velvet Underground, everyone who ate there started a hamburger chain. By 1930 dozens of chains were operating around the United States, generally as freestanding units near factories. Some, though not all, had look-alike architecture, and even misleading names, like White Tower or Royal Castle. Others, like the Chattanooga-based Krystal, or Missouri's Snappy Service, offered an identical product with a different look, such as a rounded, art deco building. It took some time for the legal ramifications of this to be sorted out, and eventually White Tower, the worst offender, was forced to kneel before the system, defrocked of its crenulated towers and left with only its name and a crippling burden of lump-sum and licensing payments. For the most part, though, the imitation went unmolested. The restaurant might be different, but the hamburger would remain the same.

There was no longer any worrying about where the meat came

from or even thinking about the sandwich at all. Hamburgers were good, and they were cheap, and the idea of buying them by the sack for a nickel apiece was so universally appealing that they came to be taken for granted. The final step in their acculturation probably came via the funny pages when, in 1931, Elzie Segar, the creator of Popeye, introduced J. Wellington Wimpy, a winning scoundrel whose great motive in life was to acquire free hamburgers. Wimpy did almost as much for hamburgers as Popeye did for spinach, though no rancher ever erected a statue to Wimpy the way the Texas spinach farmers did for Popeye. His monument instead was yet another burger chain, Wimpy's, which flourished as an overseas transplant, colonizing Great Britain, the most beef-loving of all foreign nations.

But it was in the United States, the hamburger's true home, that the sandwich really took root. America is the great icon-making nation because it requires icons more than any other nation. Created of whole cloth, peopled by immigrants from China to Peru, and with little more than a federal bureaucracy, a half-formed and contested ideology, and a common language to unite them, Americans turned to iconography again and again: first George Washington and then the Founding Fathers, and then, consecutively, the Flag, the White House, Abe Lincoln in his hat, Robert E. Lee in his uniform, Uncle Sam, the Statue of Liberty, the planting of the flag at Iwo Jima . . . the list goes on and on. And to that can be added the exemplars of American virtue, those Great Men whose lives embodied the American Way—

cultural heroes like Andrew Carnegie, Thomas Edison, Henry Ford, Charles Lindbergh, and the rest. It is no accident that popular iconography, in the form of advertising, came into its modern form here. In a country as big and vague as America, recognized symbols were, and are, at a premium.

Thus the hamburger took on its meaning. As John Jakle and Keith Sculle put it in their authoritative *Fast Food: Roadside Restaurants in the Automobile Age*, "As the first food widely available outside the traditional home, entrepreneurs serving hamburgers . . . permitted the chance for the hamburger to provide a national food for a people still in the throes of nation-building."[17] And the beauty of the hamburger, from the viewpoint of cultural history, is that unlike most other icons, it has been surprisingly supple. The limp, microscopic slider served at White Castle and its offspring looks more like a tea sandwich to us than what we think of as a hamburger. (In fact at one time, as part of Ingram's burger-gentrification scheme, Julia Joyce tried to get people to serve White Castles as tea sandwiches.) A larger, more recognizable burger appears on Coca-Cola signs in the 1930s and 1940s. Later, the familiar image of the sesame seed–topped burger, loaded with lettuce and tomato, oozing condiments, its compass points painted by right angles of yellow American cheese, shimmers into view.[18] In *The Golden Touch*, a classic Silly Symphonies cartoon directed by Walt Disney himself, Old King Midas learns the folly of his way when everything he touches turns to gold. The cracking point is when he can't eat, and in desperation the king pleads with the mischievous elf who gave him the magic touch:

KING MIDAS: Goldie, Goldie! Help me, Goldie! Take away this golden curse! Don't let me starve! Take everything! My gold, my kingdom for a hamburger sandwich!

GOLDIE: With or without onions?

KING MIDAS: Hamburger! Just plain old hamburger!

GOLDIE: Ha ha ha! Now thou art a wise and humble king.

The Golden Touch came out in 1935. By then hamburgers were an accepted piece of Americana. The incipient arrival of World War II in the late 1930s occasioned a rush of patriotism, as both isolationists and internationalists vied to show off who was more red, white, and blue. Neither of these Yankee Doodles missed the opportunity to celebrate all uniquely American institutions. How life had changed for the hamburger! Twenty years earlier, with the taint of immigration still on it, the things were being euphemized as "liberty steaks" in patriotic diners. Now readers of *Time* could learn of our boys in Egypt, where "fezzed natives were learning to fry a hamburger, and Yanks were furnishing the instructions." They could read of Walter Winchell's goodwill mission to Brazil, where the brassy Broadway columnist supposedly had "been to nightclubs only twice, but is constantly on the trail of hamburgers: 'What wouldn't I give for a hamburger?'"[19]

By the 1940s the hamburger's position in America was cemented. To celebrate America's complete triumph and vindication as the greatest democracy the world had ever seen, a spate of "national character" studies were inspired, as both academics and popular writers tried to isolate just what it was that made America great. These ranged from the anthropological, like Margaret Mead's *And Keep Your Powder Dry* (1942), to the sociological, like David Riesman's *Lonely Crowd* (1950), but all took the hamburger for granted as part of the American landscape. The reason was not that Americans liked hamburgers any more than they had previously. It was thanks to an innovation that had eluded White Castle but that helped the hamburger enter American life as a universally recognized commodity.

Consider the Big Boy icon. Although he has changed through the years, he has always stood for big sandwiches. Not just big: double size. Both gastronomically and symbolically, the hamburger took a dramatic but inevitable quantum leap in 1937, when Bob Wian added a second tier in his Glendale, California, restaurant. Wian—tall, handsome, hard working, clean-cut— was exactly the sort of person Billy Ingram imagined as the ideal White Castle operator. Wian had taken on a job washing dishes right out of high school, risen to manager, then moved to a bigger restaurant and decided he wanted his own place. He sold his

DeSoto roadster for three hundred bucks, borrowed another fifty from his father, and bought out two old ladies who owned a ten-stool hamburger stand. He was twenty-four. There were thousands of guys just like him around the country.

What catapulted Wian into food history, of course, was the confluence of two events that he had the sense to seize on and promote for the rest of his life. First, a bass player came in one night and asked for something different. Taking up the challenge, Wian took a sesame seed bun, sliced it in thirds, and proceeded to make the first designed double-decker hamburger. (This could never happen today, when all buns are presliced. Thus does innovation flourish in primitive periods.)

The sandwich was legitimately something new, because it wasn't just two patties stuck on one bun but rather something architecturally designed, and it looked like it. Wian had meant it to

Original Big Boy, 1950s Big Boy, modern Big Boy

look ridiculous, a teetering joke, but on the contrary, it looked splendidly stable. It was freaky; it looked spectacular; most of all, it was distinctive. Visually, it spoke of profusion and excess—this in the middle of the Depression, no less. It looked opulent, but it was still much cheaper than a lot of meals that were bigger and had more meat. Psychologically, though, there's something about eating a double-decker hamburger that satisfies in a way that transcends its size and weight. It's not just visual; the middle slice of bread, lacking any crust, absorbs the beef juices from the hamburgers both below and above it and quickly becomes a kind of Yorkshire pudding. The resulting richness changes the whole burger's flavor profile, adding a lushness to the sandwich's mouth-feel—an enrichment comparable to adding a smear of chili or cheese, which these burgers would also often have. The bottom line is that the hamburger had taken off into hyperspace. But what to call it?

The answer came toddling in one day in the form of Richard Woodruff, a tubby six-year-old with a huge appetite, a merry twinkle in his eye, and a pompadour haircut. He was a real boy and would do odd jobs for Wian for free food. He wore baggy jeans, and everyone called him "fat boy" affectionately. But there was a copyright on "fat boy," and so Wian decided to call his suddenly in-demand new sandwich the better, more alliterative name "Big Boy." The name is so simple that it seems almost inevitable. It was a natural, and the perfect product to be the next national food sensation.

The question confronting Bob Wian was how to make it pay. He quickly renamed his restaurant Bob's Big Boy. Unlike Walter Anderson, though, no visionary business genius appeared to transform his burger invention into a world conqueror. His realtor was just another guy. But the next best thing happened: somebody offered to give him a large sum of money for the rights to sell his Big Boy sandwich. Not the sandwich itself—that was already a public property, sold all over California in restaurants with names like Husky Boy, Chubby Boy, and Beefy Boy. What they wanted was the real deal, the actual Big Boy himself, pompadour and all. Wian was already being ripped off in California, where by 1948 he was operating three restaurants. These people were from Cincinnati and Milwaukee and West Virginia. The technical name for the arrangement they were suggesting was *franchising*. Billy Ingram had been vehemently opposed to franchising, which he felt would cheapen the White Castle brand; only the "operators" under his iron control could be counted upon to uphold the standards of the System. Wian was happy just to get a giant pile of money. He sold Big Boy rights Ohio, Kentucky, and Florida and found himself very happy simply to collect the checks.

In this way Wian allowed the immense energies of his concept to run wild. The Big Boy brand grew much faster than it ever could have if anyone had been trying to mastermind it. Even the icon itself evolved, becoming trimmer and more active as Americans became less so. If Wian didn't become a tycoon, he certainly became very rich. And he did continue to create his own units, opening six hundred before selling the business to the Marriott Corporation in 1964. Wian was now focusing on large family-style coffee shops with drive-in service *and* a large dining room. By midcentury, hamburgers and cars were as inextricable as ketchup and mustard, a trend not wasted on the California-born Wian or any of his regional rivals. Two of them, in fact, opened a drive-in burger stand in the same year as Wian, in nearby Pasadena. They had missed the boat on the Big Boy, but Maurice and Richard McDonald still believed in the burger business.

The Organization Man

McDonald's is so powerful an entity, looming so large in the eye of American life, that it's hard to believe it actually started somewhere. Its immense economic power; its vast and innumerable restaurants, in skyscrapers and food courts and pagodas, in nearly every nation; its ubiquity on radio, television, billboards, magazines, pop-up ads, movies, buses, payphones, and cell phones; its stubbornly sentimental place in the memories of three generations of Americans—all these give McDonald's an almost divine status among brands. Of course, its very size and success have, among leftists of every clime, made the company a byword for globalization and the power of creeping capital. On the other side of the spectrum, businesspeople everywhere bow to McDonald's *$41 billion* market cap, and conservatives see in the Golden Arches a vindication of the American Way. Without question it is the most symbolically loaded business in the world, and it represents America to the world in a way no other business ever has or likely ever will. As we will see, there is something profoundly American in what McDonald's is. But in the beginning, it was just another hamburger stand.

So what happened? The McDonald brothers certainly deserve a lot of credit for getting McDonald's off the ground. It's been pointed out that Ray Kroc, the founder of McDonald's, Inc., found the McDonald's system ready-made, radical and wildly successful, and deserves credit only for knowing a good thing when he saw one. That is true, but misleading. The McDonald's burger stand in San Bernardino was a technical innovation almost on par with the first White Castle. Richard and Maurice McDonald, like everybody else, were running drive-in stands by the seat of their pants—first a hot dog stand in Pasadena and then a "drive-in burger bar" in San Bernardino in 1940. The brothers just happened to be better at it than their competitors. They were unfailingly hard working, but that went without saying about people operating marginal businesses at the tail end of the Great Depression. They were also imaginative: both Richard and Maurice were constantly tinkering with the process, thinking about how to make hot dogs and hamburgers more efficiently. More than anyone else the McDonalds can be said to have made the Model T of food, systematizing the process to a degree that Billy Ingram might have envied. But neither man was a visionary, and neither had that profound devotion to systemic conformity that, among the true titans of hamburger history, rose to an almost religious conviction.

Essentially, events forced their hand. The McDonalds had it good in the early 1940s, making money hand over fist at the popular drive-in. The place featured twenty nubile young carhops, who, though slow as molasses, brought a lot of business in. Their stainless steel, octagonal building, transparent on all sides, allowed customers to see how clean the place was—always a concern in the hamburger business. Nor were hamburgers their only product: the featured item on the menu of the first McDonald's wasn't a hamburger at all but barbecue items slow-smoked with hickory chips trucked in from Arkansas.

Nonetheless, problems plagued the operation. Some were universal in the restaurant business. In 1940 restaurants paid out on average 27 percent of their gross income as wages. But once veterans flooded the marketplace after World War II, the figure was significantly higher, in the 35–40 percent range. And then as now, jobs in fast food were considered among the worst you could find. Who can forget Dana Andrews's humiliating job as a soda jerk in William Wyler's *The Best Years of Our Lives* (1946)? And soda jerk was a prestige position compared to that of a fry cook or carhop. As a result, the brothers were hostage to the caprices of teenagers and the reliability of drunks.

And then there was a larger problem. McDonald's was a new kind of business, catering to the changes in American society activated by the coming of the automobile age. Everywhere in

America, and especially in California, people were more mobile, less formal, more in need of quick and easy meals that could be eaten on the go. One reason the hamburger so far outstripped its rivals in the fast-food era was because it was so easy to eat a burger while driving. (Try to consume barbecue behind the wheel sometime.) Along with a lot of other restaurateurs, the McDonalds had accommodated car culture and in so doing had risen on an updraft of progress. But the change didn't happen all at once, and the place was still burdened by the customs of preautomotive dining: knives, forks, plates, a big menu, slow-smoked meats, and all the rest of it.[1] The carhops were an appealing novelty, but they, too, compromised the restaurant, attracting good-for-nothing teenage boys who would loiter around and not order anything. Worst of all, the service was slow. More than anything else, the McDonalds understood that, in the fast-food business, the food that was fastest was best. "We'd say to ourselves there has to be a faster way," Richard McDonald would remember years later. "The cars were jamming up the lot. Customers weren't demanding it, but our intuition told us they would like speed. Everything was moving faster. The supermarkets and dime stores had already converted to self-service, and it was obvious the future of drive-ins was self-service."[2]

It may or may not have been obvious to other drive-in owners. Yet what made the brothers' fortune was not their intuition but the fact that they had the stones to tear down a successful business, monkeying with a good thing. The restaurant, for all its problems, was still making them a lot of money, and despite its manifest inefficiencies, nobody had come up with anything better. Hamburgers were still being made in the White Castle mode, albeit with a way of accommodating cars.

The McDonalds knew they could do better and were willing to lose money trying. This alone entitles them to a place in hamburger lore. Their remedy was radical: in 1948 they closed the place down, fired all the carhops, and completely redesigned the way the restaurant was run. The dishwasher also got notice: there would be no flatware, no glasses, no tableware at all. Everything would be made of paper or plastic. And despite all the labor and capital they had sunk into it, they gave barbecue the heave-ho, too. ("The more we hammered away at the barbecue business, the more hamburgers we sold," Richard McDonald later remembered.)[3] They pared the menu down to hamburgers, cheeseburgers, sodas, milk, coffee, potato chips, and pie.

The brothers had it in their mind to rationalize completely the hamburger-making process, to create an assembly-line system that Detroit would be proud of. The business the brothers were envisioning wasn't just a quicker hamburger stand, it was an entirely new kind of business, and they knew it. If a fifteen-cent hamburger could be ready as soon as someone wanted it; if it was a high-quality, reliable item sold at a good price; if the customer neither had to wait nor tip; and, best of all, if you could get rid of the customer in the time it took to exchange the money, the making and selling of hamburgers could become a continuous process. McDonald's had always been a volume business, but it was a stop-and-start operation, riddled with downtime and waste. This was to be a continuous process, one that could accommodate a constant flow of customers: essentially, a profit machine that you would turn on in the morning and turn off at night.

Here was the American dream at its best: a kind of aesthetic cupidity, profit-making mixed with unfettered inventiveness in the service of a product nobody had the slightest regard for. The brothers took feverish pleasure in refining the system down to the last decimal. They had the staff pantomime the making of hamburgers on their tennis court, tracing out the steps as you would at a dance school—a veritable minuet of meat. And when a rare rain came along and washed away all the steps, they just did it all over again. "Richard handled the project," his nephew Ronald McDonald would later write, "like a general planning a full-scale war. He covered every detail of kitchen operation and even counted the actual steps the employees would have to take to use the equipment."[4]

And what about that equipment? Clearly the standard apparatus wouldn't do if the leading edge of hamburger progress were to move forward. First, that meant standardizing the morphology of the hamburger just as White Castle had done. Richard McDonald interviewed candy manufacturers to find out what kind of machine they used to form peppermint patties; he found a lever-operated device that could press them out with one pull.

To cook his burgers, he would need a big grilling surface—much larger than any on the market. The largest griddles then being made were three feet long; McDonald commissioned a machinist to create two six-foot griddles, each big enough for three men to stand side by side at, cooking dozens and dozens of hamburgers at a time. The machinist, Ed Toman, went into a prolonged trance of inspiration and created one new tool after another, none of which (unfortunately for him) was ever patented: a stainless steel lazy Susan, on which buns might rest, awaiting the just-finished burgers as they came off the griddle; a condiment pump that would squirt just the right amount of ketchup or mustard on a burger with one pump; and of course, like White Castle, a bigger, stronger spatula to handle all that pressing and flipping. Finally, since the linchpin of the whole plan was to have burgers ready the second people ordered them, a system was invented to keep the burgers warm with a "heat bar" powered by heated metal Calrods, the industry standard. (Later, befitting a space-age operation, McDonald's would switch to infrared beams.) Another system dictated when the burgers had been sitting around too long and should be discarded.

When the dust had settled and the Great Machine had finally opened to the public, the response was . . . indifference. Drivers honked for carhops who would never again come. Disgusted, they drove away. A few even hectored the brothers, asking, "You're really swamped, aren't you?" A directive went out to the staff to park in the lot so that it would look as though McDonald's had some business. What if you invented the greatest hamburger business in the world and nobody came? Such was the quandry put to the McDonald brothers. But, as they knew it would, virtue was eventually rewarded, and McDonald's became a powerhouse. Soon lines were snaking into the parking lot. In 1951 the place was making $277,000 a year, 40 percent than its wildly successful former self. By the mid-1950s, Richard and Maurice McDonald were seeing $100,000 in profits every year and trading in their Cadillacs annually. Their gamble had paid off, in the only way that mattered.

And it wasn't just the money. The restaurant was a spectacular success in the most literal sense. Word of McDonald's phenomenal triumph had gotten around the southern California hamburger community, and businessmen were going there just to watch the money machine at work, humming profitably away. "I have never seen anything as breathtaking since then," James Collins, the head of Sizzler restaurants, would later tell David Halberstam. "There was a line of people halfway out to the curb and the parking lot was full. There was nothing else like it. They had two hamburger lines and they were handling people every ten seconds. I tore up my coffee shop plans and entered the hamburger business, and except for the fact that I sold hamburgers for 19 cents, everything else was the same as McDonald's."[5]

Things only intensified when *American Restaurant* magazine

put McDonald's on the cover of its July 1952 issue. The headline was low on subtlety: "One Million Hamburgers and 160 Tons of French Fries a Year." This message, combined with the magic figure of 17 percent labor costs, thrilled entrepreneurs, who responded as avidly as teenagers stumbling across a copy of *Penthouse* in the attic. They hastened McDonald's-ward. One of these visitors was the incredulous president of the company who made their milkshake machines. The man could not believe that they were using eight of his heavy-duty Multimixers at a time; even the busiest ice cream fountains needed just one or two.

What Ray Kroc found astounded him. His memoir, *Grinding It Out*, is surprisingly revealing about Kroc's personality. Written in his emeritus years, it was his valediction, and intended to justify McDonald's ways to man. Though filled with salesman's mottos ("It is no achievement to walk a tightrope laid flat on the floor") and depression-generation nostrums ("Work is the meat in the hamburger of life"), it also gives us a long glimpse into Kroc's volcanic emotional life. The book is poetic and paradoxical in a way you would not expect a ghostwritten corporate memoir to be, and never more so than at the decisive hour when Ray Kroc first visits McDonald's. Kroc is checking out the San Bernardino operation, noting admiringly the long lines, the spotless kitchen, the busy staff in their "spiffy white shirts and trousers," "bustling around like ants at a picnic." Eight Multimixers blazed away, and Kroc stood in line, dazed at the efficiency and vitality of the place. Then Kroc saw his symbol of the future: the archetypal California blonde, symbol of the West. Sitting in a yellow convertible, the woman was "demolishing a hamburger . . . with a demure precision that was fascinating." Kroc approached her.[6]

> "If you don't mind telling me, how often do you come here?" I asked. "Anytime I am in the neighborhood," she smiled. "And that's as often as possible, because my boy-friend lives here." Whether she was teasing or being can-did or simply using the mention of her boyfriend as a ploy to discourage this inquisitive middle-aged guy who might be a masher, I couldn't tell, and I cared not at all. It was not her sex appeal but the obvious relish with which she devoured the hamburger that made my pulse begin to hammer with excitement. Her appetite was magnified by the many people in cars that filled the parking lot, and I could feel myself getting wound up like a pitcher with a no-hitter going. This had to be the most amazing mer-chandising operation I had ever seen![7]

Kroc was at this time fifty-two, a successful businessman after thirty years of excruciating effort. In all that time, he never had found a vehicle he could really ride. McDonald's, he knew, was his own yellow convertible, a once-in-a-lifetime opportunity he couldn't let pass by. He had made such farsighted decisions be-fore. He had given up a good job selling paper cups when he re-alized that the machines that mixed the shakes in the cup, not the cups themselves, were the real winners. Now he saw that it was not the mixers but the shakes, and the hamburgers, and the french fries, that had created this commotion in the middle of a desert. Without hesitating, he went up to the McDonald brothers and proposed that they make him their national franchising agent. That was okay with the McDonalds. They were already trying to promote their "Speedee Service System," but only in the most haphazard way. When someone suggested to them that he wanted to open a McDonald's in Arizona, they were incredulous. "Who's heard of us in Arizona?" they asked.

The McDonalds didn't have the temperament, the world-beating, domineering, Napoleonic outlook that was Kroc's special genius; they were the operational pioneers, the Walter Andersons to his Billy Ingram. What they lacked in ambition he had, as he might have put it, in spades. They had their yearly Cadillacs, their swimming pool, their much-deserved ease after their own thirty-year odyssey. They didn't have wives or kids. They just wanted to enjoy their money. Ray Kroc did have a wife and a child and a company of his own: but he risked it all to pursue his dream.

Of what did this dream consist? Kroc saw it from the first: "Visions of McDonald's restaurants dotting crossroads all over the country paraded through my brain."[8] Kroc saw all at once what McDonald's would become. It was his dream that made it a reality, and he, more than the McDonald brothers, is the true author of McDonald's success. Admittedly, they created the assembly-line hamburger operation, its Gutenberg press, and in that sense are the inventors of modern fast food; and Harry Sonneborn, the financial architect of the business, created the unique mortgage arrangement that turned the company into a global powerhouse. But McDonald's as we know it today was purely a product of Kroc's personality, which was supremely American in a way few of either his critics or his admirers appreciate.

He was a flawed, troubled man, famously difficult, irascible, intolerant, narrow. He would rage at employees for not retrieving unused ketchup packets or allowing hamburger wrappers to be seen in the parking lot. Nor were his own most trusted advisers and lieutenants free from the tyranny of his caprices. One lawyer was fired for wearing a knit hat to work on a freezing Chicago day; others were summarily dismissed, or at the least dressed down in a red-faced fury in front of their coworkers, for violating one or another of his endless, arbitrary anathemas: bubble gum, white socks, pipes, uncombed hair, sport coats, the drinking of Manhattans, nose hairs, beards, moustaches, sideburns. Frequently, his kindhearted secretary–underboss June Martino would save Kroc from himself, humoring him until his mood passed and thus saving some poor soul's job.

In matters of thrift, he was just as overbearing. Senior managers who had built McDonald's from the ground up had to listen to his lectures and letters on household economy, such as where the best sales were or what budget-saving household tips might benefit the ideal McDonald's wife. Even by the standards of the 1950s, he was dogmatic and parochial. He despised not only intellectuals and artists but also corporate loafers and country club bigwigs—no one but his own stripe of self-willed entrepreneur seemed to merit his respect. He was a titan of bad vibrations: when Kroc bought the San Diego Padres at age seventy, he introduced himself on the team's public address system by calling out the players as losers during a packed home game. Predictably, he approached business as total war, and he rejoiced in his pitilessness: "If they were drowning, I'd put a hose in their mouth," he once said of his rivals.[9]

If ever someone were cast as The Man, the living symbol and soul of everything the baby boom generation hated, it was Kroc. He was a square's square. Hostility oozed from his pores; he was the apotheosis of the Protestant work ethic, sublimating all frustration and unhappiness into greater competitive fury. "This is rat eat rat, dog eat dog," he told a reporter in 1972. "I'll kill 'em before they kill me. You're talking about the American way of survival of the fittest."[10] That same year, he gave a quarter of a million dollars to Richard Nixon's reelection campaign. He was buttoned-down, squared-away, filled with rage and repression, and single-minded in his lifelong pursuit of capitalism. Everything about him suggested a classic Depression-era control freak. No man could have been more uptight.

And yet—and here was his genius—when it came to advancing the cause of McDonaldizing the world, he was flexible and open-minded. For all his nostrums and mottoes, and the prejudices he so pugnaciously asserted, when it came to running the business that was his life's love and work, Kroc was supremely supple. Because he was so single-mindedly committed to Mc-Donald's ("my personal monument to capitalism"), Kroc had an almost Buddha-like disregard of his own ego. Everything about his management style was inclusive and absorptive; he picked men who were totally opposed to him in character and temperament and gave them complete carte blanche to run essential aspects of McDonald's as they saw fit. Fred Turner, one of Kroc's first hires, was told on his first day of work that "you have to work with your suit coat on, and there is no smoking at your desk." Within an hour, Turner had his sleeves rolled up and a cigarette going. Kroc said nothing. "If his managers were contributing to building *his* McDonald's, there were on his side—no matter how much their personalities differed from his," writes John Love in *McDonald's: Behind the Arches*, the best study of the company. "Kroc not only tolerated such frustrations, he set himself up for them by hiring people who had personal traits he knew would upset him." That didn't matter, though. What mattered was McDonald's.[11]

Which is not to say that he did not get upset. Kroc was temperamentally and philosophically opposed, with every fiber of his being, to the kind of dissent that he found necessary for the company's success. He knew what was best for McDonald's. And yet the company's immense success would not have been possible had Kroc run it in the autocratic way he sometimes seemed to desire. When it came to franchisees, dissent was especially unthinkable, a cancer that needed to be excised with the sharpest knife. Speaking of headstrong operators, he had this to say, in a highly Nixonian taped message to the McDonald brothers: "We have found out as you have that we cannot trust some people who are nonconformists. We will make conformists out of them in a hurry. . . . They can have no alternative whatsoever. You can't give them an inch. The organization cannot trust the individual; the individual must trust the organization or he shouldn't go into this kind of business."[12]

And yet it was a franchisee who invented the Big Mac, a franchisee who invented the Egg McMuffin, a franchisee who invented the point-of-sale protocol ("May I have your order, please?"). A franchisee invented Ronald McDonald! Franchisees have conceived and developed most of the marketing and product innovations that have propelled McDonald's to fast-food supremacy. Far from being mindless "conformists," these imaginative, dedicated entrepreneurs were cut in Kroc's mold and served as his proxies and police. He could never have imposed himself on so many independent businesspeople, no matter how draconian the lease arrangement or legal contract; yet like barbarian tribes who, being conquered by the Romans, become Roman themselves, the McDonald's system spread virally, powered by the very forces of individual initiative that Kroc adored and detested. The same went for senior management. "If two executives think the same, one of them is superfluous," was an axiom he was found of quoting.

This paradox, this dynamic, discordant, richly generative tension between conformity and initiative, is the secret to the company's success. It is no accident that McDonald's is the most iconic American business in the world. It is the business that most participates in America's essential nature. McDonald's is not the result of one man's quirks in how he approached his employees. Kroc embodied and transmitted the genius, not of the Speedee Service System, nor even of the McDonald's System, but rather of the vast and contradictory energies of the American System, of which he was the consummate product. "Ray Kroc, Embodiment of Mid-Twentieth Century America," is the title of one tribute.[13] The statement is too qualified.

Conformity, it will be remembered, was a serious social issue in the 1950s. In the wake of World War II, America suddenly found itself as the real, and not just imagined, beacon of all the nations. All at once, solemn studies of what was then called "our national character" began to appear. These varied greatly but were generally positive. Even books like Gunnar Myrdal's *American Dilemma* (1944) and Will Herberg's *Protestant-Catholic-Jew* (1955), which looked, respectively, at race and religion in critical terms, agreed that America was singularly harmonious and a model for consensus abroad. "Consensus" in fact became a major intellectual shibboleth in the postwar years: historian John

Higham, writing in 1962, saw a veritable "cult of consensus" in the work of historians like Daniel Boorstin and Richard Hofstatder whose influential books celebrated Americans' mythic ability to get along.[14]

The postwar era of good feelings didn't last long, though. Throughout the decade, a number of dissenting studies appeared, stressing the stultifying, soul-deadening power of conformity. Americans, it was said, had lost every bit of their independence and constituted a "lonely crowd," in the words of sociologist David Riesman. Insecure and "other directed," contemporary Americans had replaced their internal gyroscope with a set of sensitive social antennae and shuffled mindlessly from a home that was essentially a prison (John Keats's *Crack in the Picture Window*, 1956) via a car that actually drove them (*The Insolent Chariots*, 1958, also by Keats) and arrived at a workplace in which the slightest show of individuality was verboten (C. Wright Mills's *White Collar*, 1951; Sloane Wilson's *Man in the Gray Flannel Suit*, 1955; William Whyte's *Organization Man*, 1956). Women were even more imprisoned, but that fact wasn't discovered until the early 1960s.

Of all the studies, *The Organization Man* was probably the most influential, in part because it was written from inside the system. Unlike academics like Mills and Riesman, Whyte was an editor at *Fortune*, and his study, which drew on hundreds of interviews of corporate executives, bore no ideological opposition to capitalism or business. Whyte was primarily concerned with the trend, not because it degraded humanity or promoted an unjust class system, but because he saw it as sapping America's strength, particularly in business. "This book is not a plea for nonconformity. . . . I am not, accordingly, addressing myself to the surface uniformities of U.S. life," he wrote. "There will be no strictures in this book against 'Mass Man'—a person the author has never met—nor will there be any strictures against ranch wagons, or television sets, or gray flannel suits." Business was now just about getting ahead by getting along—at the cost of the energies that had built America. "Within business there are still many who cling resolutely to the Protestant Ethic, and some with as much rapacity as drove any nineteenth-century buccaneer. But only rarely are they of The Organization," Whyte wrote, regretfully. He had never heard of Ray Kroc.[15]

At McDonald's the organization was never a top-down structure, Kroc's choleric outbursts notwithstanding. By all outward appearances, it should have been a hotbed of conformity, an incubator of Organization Men. But nearly the opposite was true. Though monolithic from the outside, with a branding strategy that seems to hint at transnational brainwashing, McDonald's is not, strictly speaking, a hamburger corporation at all. It is a confederation of entrepreneurs, small businesspeople operating according to standards devised by a central organizing authority. McDonald's does own a large number of its own restaurants, but this was a late development in the company's history and, though highly profitable, a departure from Ray Kroc's dream.

Kroc, like Billy Ingram, was a visionary, at least by business standards. Though he lacked the White Castle founder's flair, Kroc was a deeper thinker, a true ideologue. He was at first excited by the McDonald's system because he realized that, in his fifties, he had at last found the product worthy of his God-given sales skills, the vehicle he could ride to riches after thirty years of selling paper cups and blenders. But soon he began to see in McDonald's a way for entrepreneurs like himself—simple, hardworking people with little or no higher education—to multiply and be fruitful. McDonald's was the wave of the future: thanks to the postwar boom and the National Highway Act, America was becoming an automobile-based society, and McDonald's would be its ideal fueling station, especially in the new suburbs springing up everywhere. These suburbs, a long-promised paradise of the American middle class, where every industrious man could at long last own a house and a car, even at a working man's salary, was an America of young families and high hopes, and the areas they were moving to were blank slates from a restaurant standpoint, ready to be writ upon by McDonald's. It was the wave of the future, all right, and Kroc wanted the hustlers, the strivers, the People That Made America Great to surf it alongside him. For him, McDonald's would be the great fulfillment of the America Dream, the ultimate vindication of free enterprise. "Our slogan for McDonald's operators is, 'in business for yourself, but not by yourself,' and it is one of the secrets to our success," Kroc would later write. McDonald's operators were sometimes astounded to find out how passionate Kroc was about entrepreneurial ideology. He was a capitalist Lenin. Once, faced with a blatantly illegal attempt by a rival chain to undersell his McDonald's, suggested to Kroc that they might initiate legal action. Kroc replied, or remembers having replied, as follows: "I'm going to tell you something I feel very strongly about. The thing that has made this country great is our free enterprise system. If we have to resort to this—bringing in the government—to beat our competition, then we deserve to go broke. If we can't do it by offering a better fifteen-cent hamburger, by being better merchandisers, by providing faster services and a cleaner place, than I would rather be broke tomorrow and out of this business and start all over again in something else."[16]

Kroc's commitment to the individual operators of McDonald's was more than philosophical. In the truest language he was capable of speaking, he put their interests ahead of his own, allowing them to get rich while he (and McDonald's, Inc.) stayed barely solvent.

Franchising was the secret to McDonald's success, and the secret to the company's soul, the wellspring from which it grew. There would be much talk later about McDonald's being a real estate company rather a hamburger business, and there was some truth to that, as we'll see. But it was in the concept of cooperative partnership between the company and its franchisees that tapped into the boundless economic energies of the postwar years and helped McDonald's to take its place at the center of American commercial culture. *Time* grasped this, writing in 1969 of the franchising boom: "The system thrives because it combines the incentive of personal ownership—the best goad man has yet devised to spur hard work—with the managerial talents of big business."[17] Personal ownership and Big Business, the best of both worlds. McDonald's represented the best that America had to offer.

Not that there was anything new about franchising: the concept had been invented in the nineteenth century by the Singer Sewing Machine company and was subsequently taken up by a number of automobile manufacturers. It was an ingenious system for building a business without a lot of capital: the franchiser got a network of dealers, and the dealers got a ready-to-sell product, complete with brand recognition and (it was hoped) a good reputation. In practice, however, most franchising operations were simply a cashbox for the franchiser. He had created a successful business, so let the other guy pay him off if he wanted to piggyback on his name. Certainly this was how the McDonald brothers thought of it. (Richard: "When this hit all over the country . . . we knew that we had something that was going to make us some money.")[18] Typically, a business would sell territorial franchise rights so that the franchisee would have a lock on the region.

This didn't make sense to Kroc. The franchisees had to be

kept in line somehow, and if the corporation was doling out territorial franchises, it would have no control over individual restaurants. So McDonald's, it was decided, would franchise individual restaurants via twenty-year leases. If the franchisees didn't hold up the McDonald's name, they would lose the lease. Kroc also had the foresight to see that McDonald's would flourish only if the franchisees made money. So he sold the franchises as the McDonald's franchising agent for the rock-bottom price of nine hundred dollars. But he was adamant that the franchisees hew to the McDonald's operating system, regarding the slightest variation as an act of industrial espionage. (It was in one moment of such frustration that Kroc had told the McDonald brothers, "We cannot trust some people who are nonconformists. We will make conformists out of them in a hurry.")[19]

It was a serious problem. Once someone paid franchise fees— for a marginal business, moreover, with little fame outside southern California—they not unreasonably felt it was their right to run it as they chose. After all, it was their life savings on the line, their mortgages and second mortgages and in-law loans at stake, not Ray Kroc's, with his endless book of rules and regulations. But from Kroc's point of view, these variations jeopardized the whole enterprise. It wasn't just that the brand's value would be diluted; inevitably, he felt, as franchisees faced tough times, they would resort to cost-cutting measures, resulting in gnarly hamburgers, limp french fries, sloppy restaurants, and worse. Unthinkable! It was for this reason that Billy Ingram had steadfastly

refused to permit White Castle to be franchised, even after Mc-
Donald's and the other burger chains were expanding at an unprecedented rate. To this day, every White Castle is an outpost
of the parent corporation, and its managers and staff are corporate employees. (It is also the reason why White Castle, despite
its thirty-year head start, is a stable and solvent but relatively tiny
chain today.)

Moreover, the kind of control Kroc wanted on an operational
level (french fries made from carefully cured potatoes, spotless
building exteriors, a seventy-five-page manual beginning, "Here-
in outlined is *the* successful method . . .") ran against the grain of
the kind of people he wanted for the McDonald's "family." Early
on Kroc had sold franchises to his immediate circle, country club
friends dazzled by his promise of big profits. But these affluent
men and women lacked the desire to spend twenty hours a day
running a hamburger restaurant as if their lives depended on it.
Because in fact their lives didn't depend on it. They knew Kroc
only because they shared his haute bourgeois success. His dream
of a hamburger stand run like the Rolls Royce plant had no
magic for them. What Kroc needed, really needed, were people
like Sandy and Betty Agate.

The Agates were the prototypical early McDonald's franchisees. Kroc fell in love with the Agates when Betty stopped in
at the office one day, selling Catholic Bibles door-to-door. In
conversation with June Martino, Kroc's secretary and the informal matriarch of McDonald's, it came out that Betty was Jewish.

"What the hell is a Jew doing selling Catholic Bibles?" Martino asked. "Making a living," Betty Agate replied. "Why don't you get a McDonald's instead?" Martino asked. The Agates did. They were the people Kroc had been thinking of all along. A printer who had gone to night school to get a degree in optometry, Sandy Agate managed somehow to get the $950 together for a franchise. Betty Agate was behind him all the way. "Let's reach for the moon," she told her husband as they drove home from Kroc's house after the sales pitch. The Agates, Kroc's first successful franchisers in the Midwest, opened their store in Waukegan, Illinois, in May 1955. It was an immediate success. Soon the Agates were making four times as much as Kroc himself. But Kroc wasn't primarily concerned with money by that time in his life, except of course as a way to promote the gospel of McDonald's, so that made him even happier. He now had a franchise he could point to, an example of the McDonald's gold mine in action.

The story of Sandy Agate, however, doesn't end happily. (Arguably, the same could be said of the McDonald's Corporation or for that matter America.) Though commendably hardworking and a model franchisee in so many ways, Agate was not temperamentally suited to buckling under to Kroc. He was "his own man," as he told his wife. If he wasn't, he would have settled in to his life as a printer instead of risking everything on a hamburger stand. McDonald's began to identify Agate, over several years, as a problem operator. He didn't follow the directions to the letter.

He insisted on expressing his own will. The breaking point came when Agate switched his store over to Pepsi from Coke. A more perfect illustration of the tension between entrepreneurs and corporations could hardly be found. McDonald's was an aspiring franchise corporation and had made a deal with an established franchise corporation, Coca-Cola, to supply its restaurants. There was no room in that equation for the needs or desires of individual McDonald's owners, any more than there was for local bottlers. The deal was made on the corporate level. Then Agate was offered some inducement by the local Pepsi bottler to switch. He did, and Ray Kroc never forgave him.

Kroc's position was understandable. Not only was it a flagrant challenge to his authority, but it was counterproductive. One of the great advantages McDonald's operators had over their rivals was that the corporation, unlike most franchisers, didn't sell supplies to franchisees at a profit; it used its great buying power to get them a good price, which it then passed on without taking a cent.

Agate was his own man, but it cost him additional franchises, and when the twenty-year franchise lease was up, he left the Mc-Donald's family for good. This then was the crux of the conformity problem, the central paradox of McDonald's business and, really, of much of cultural life in the 1950s. The liberal consensus was tolerant and productive, and everybody seemed to agree that it was a distinctly American invention. From the diverse "bomber crew" clichés that mark the movies of the 1950s to the homilies penned by intellectuals in *Partisan Review*, the idea was that we had figured out how to create unity in diversity, unlike Russia or Nazi Germany, where everybody was expected to act exactly the same, or else. McDonald's, like America, was meant to create "out of many, one." But there were very real limits to the freedom conformity conferred, even if boom times and atom-age anxiety kept them at arm's length for a while.

As it happened, though, the corporate society, as it turned out, was equipped with vents; the history of the next thirty years demonstrated how easily American corporate culture was able to absorb the shocks of the 1960s. Money and property, as everyone now knows, turned out to be reconcilable with personal freedom and creativity—to an extent. You can call your boss by his or her first name and wear casual clothes to work, but he or she is still your boss and you have to show up and do your job. At McDonald's the dream of freedom administered to franchisees came in the form of marketing. If you owned a McDonald's, you had to do everything by the book. But if you thought it might help business, you could come up with new slogans, new offers, new ads, even new products—and in fact, nearly every new product that McDonald's has introduced, with the exception of Chicken McNuggets, has been created by a local franchisee: the Big Mac in Pittsburgh by Jim Delligatti, an alumnus of the original Bob's Big Boy in Glendale; breakfast, also by Delligatti; the Egg McMuffin, by Herb Peterson of Santa Barbara, which made breakfast a success; the Filet-O-Fish, by Lou Groen in Cincinnati, home to many Catholics who wouldn't eat meat on Friday. More important, the franchisees had free rein in promoting McDonald's. Most important, this meant television advertising, which was practically the central nervous system of the suburbs McDonald's was moving to—sprawling, isolated communities where television was virtually the only plane of contact among residents.

Today it's impossible to think of McDonald's apart from its omnipotent brand identity and the decades of television and print advertising that have imprinted it on our minds. That is because McDonald's developed along with television; both are pillars of postwar American life. Ronald McDonald, the personality-free clown whom, if a McDonald's-sponsored study is to be believed, 96 percent of American schoolchildren can identify, began his life as a local Bozo the Clown entertaining Washington, DC, toddlers on a local television station. These baby boomers were McDonald's target customers, and local franchisees John Gibson and Oscar Goldstein hired the guy who played Bozo, Willard Scott (later the *Today Show* weatherman), to play the clown full-time. Ronald would eventually become the star of a national advertising campaign paid for by the collective franchisees, each of whom donated 1 percent of sales to support it. Eventually the commercials would become inseparable from the success of McDonald's in the minds of many. But Ronald McDonald, like the Big Mac, was a grass-roots phenomenon. The ease with which McDonald's, as a national entity, assimilated it attests to the seamlessness of the system. McDonald's, by the early 1960s, had become a mechanism of such surpassing absorptive power that to this day, almost no place on earth has had the power of resisting it. In the republic of McDonald's, all franchises are in it together, moving forward and sharing in the vast and inevitable further prosperity of McDonald's.

This, then, was the ultimate triumph of Ray Kroc: a society of McDonald's franchisees, all living according to established, company-set standards of Quality, Service, Cleanliness, and Value, producing hamburgers of 1.6 ounces, of 100 percent ground chuck, formed into a patty of 3 and 5/8ths inches in diameter. The McDonald's hamburger, which made so many strivers rich, was juicy, with a fat content between 17 and 20 percent, and was served with a quarter ounce of onion, a teaspoon of mustard, a tablespoon of ketchup, and a pickle 1 inch in diameter. And it sat on an enriched white bun, pillowy and ethereal, to which a little sugar was added in order to make it caramelize better when toasted. It always had to be the same. The franchisees, obedient and prosperous, and with a free hand in promoting their stores, existed on a plane of dynamic, point-of-service action that, to the outside, seemed the whole story of McDonald's. What was McDonald's, after all, except a well-run hamburger chain? Closer inspection might reveal the utopian or Soviet aspects of the franchising system, but that still didn't explain the singular success of the Golden Arches. In fact, there were two planes sandwiching the business as it could be observed by the naked eye, the buns to the hamburger of McDonald's visible business.

One was the exacting, minutely detailed operations system created by the McDonald brothers and then expanded and perfected by McDonald's operations chief Fred Turner. McDonald's, from the first, was famous for the absolute consistency that the chain demonstrated in nearly every location. This was no accident. The manual told every employee exactly where to stand, what to do, and precisely which stimuli required what response. Flashing lights, timers, and buzzers kept the staff's judgment calls to a minimum; essentially they were space monkeys, easily replaceable if they goofed off, talked back, or tried to unionize. Even if they didn't, they tended not to stay on the job very long. McDonald's tended to hire teenagers, not veteran cooks. Teenagers, especially baby boom teenagers, tended to live at home. They quit the job when they felt like it and were replaced by someone just like them. The key was the system. Grill men knew that they had to put hamburgers down on the grill in double file from left to right. The third row got the most heat, so it was to be flipped first, followed by the fourth, fifth, and sixth, followed by the two left-most burgers. They all came off at the same time, and then somebody else dressed them, to equally robotic rhythms. As for management, they all had to complete a rigorous training at Hamburger University, the official academy of the McDonald's system.

Theodore Leavitt, a professor at Harvard Business School, has written an especially keen and sinister appreciation of McDonald's system. According to him, "A McDonald's retail outlet is a machine that produces a highly polished product. Through painstaking attention to total design and facilities planning, everything is built integrally into the machine itself, into the technology of the system. *The only choice available to the attendant is to operate it exactly as the designers intended.*"[20]

This passage explains everything that people distrust about McDonald's but is also why they take its supreme reliability for granted. Yet something about it seems dehumanizing. There's little to like about a hyperrationalized kitchen from an employee's, or for that matter a customer's, point of view—much nostalgia and affection still abided, even in the 1950s, for the familiar grill man, chatting with customers as he flipped burgers and taking pleasure in his work. But from a business point of view, the system was invaluable. It made McDonald's predictable and productive, and a veritable moneymaking machine in the best franchises. And money was the other aspect to the company's rise and the one that remains the least understood when talking about McDonald's.

Finance, even more than operations, was the secret side of the company's success. McDonald's, from a business standpoint, could be said to have two founding fathers. The one the company celebrates, and rightly, is Ray Kroc. (The McDonald brothers appear only as dim and mythic figures, the Romulus and Remus of the McDonald's empire.) You don't hear as much about Harry Sonneborn; but in his way he is every bit as important as Kroc.

Harry Sonneborn was not an unforgettable character. There

are no colorful maxims attached to his name, no memorable anecdotes. A cold, distant martinet with a military haircut and a laser focus on the ledger sheet, he was the epitome of the heartless moneyman. Sonneborn had no particular interest in hamburgers. He could just as easily have been the financial architect of Microsoft or McDonnell Douglas. On the Mount Rushmore of hamburgers, where are sculpted the great hamburger men, there is no place for him alongside the visages of Walter Anderson, Billy Ingram, Ray Kroc, and Dave Thomas. But in his own way he was every bit as bold and far-sighted as any of them. In the 1950s and 1960s, there were a lot of burger chains, as we will see in the next chapter. There was Burger Chef, Burger King, Burger Queen, Wimpy's, White Castle and its clones, not to mention Bob Wian's scattered offspring. But there is only one McDonald's. Why? Because the hamburgers were so much better? Because the kitchen was run by scientific management? Because Ronald McDonald was such a compelling comic figure? No. McDonald's became what it is for two reasons. One, because it was the first and the best hamburger franchise restaurant, with the most far-sighted senior management. And two, because Harry Sonneborn figured out a way to finance a multibillion-dollar empire without cash, collateral, or even a significant show of profitability. The mainsprings of McDonald's success, which he engineered, were intricate and invisible, and more powerful than anyone at the time could have imagined.

Kroc's vision for McDonald's was predicated on motivated,

small-time individual franchisees, hungry for the chance to join others like themselves in the race for success. But the problem with those franchisees was that they didn't have much money. How would they purchase the land, build the actual store, and outfit it with equipment? And once having done so, what could McDonald's do, short of refusing them further franchises, to keep their "nonconformity" in check? As the experience with the Agates had shown, the very thing that made a man an entrepreneur made him unsuitable as an obedient "operator." Sonneborn at one stroke solved both problems. McDonald's would convince a local property owner to build a McDonald's and lease it to the company—which would then lease it to the franchisee at a 40 percent markup. The company thus had the power to expand without capital, control over the franchisee, and, most important, a much-needed source of revenue—one that was impervious to sales, the economy, or even the quality of the franchisee. This single invention is at the heart of McDonald's success. Because the arrangement was so tidy and profitable, Sonneborn was able to borrow massive amounts of capital from institutions, such as giant life insurance companies, which otherwise looked askance at "fast food" as an investment. Sonneborn would frequently go so far as to tell investors that McDonald's was a real estate company, not a hamburger company. "Viewed coldly and narrowly from a numbers perspective, there is more truth to Sonneborn's remark about real estate than anyone at McDonald's cares to acknowledge," John Love later wrote.[21]

Thanks to Sonneborn's innovation, McDonald's was positioned to keep expanding. McDonald's got ownership of the land and the property without using any of its own money. It took some doing, but Sonneborn got all the cash McDonald's needed from institutional investors that would be completely immune to either Kroc's sales pitch or his ideological fervor. McDonald's now rode on the tides of macroeconomics: leveraged in the extreme, it had a mechanism for making money that completely transcended hamburgers.

Kroc, for his part, was delirious. "I have finally found the way," he told the McDonald brothers in early 1957, "that will put every single McDonald's we open under our complete control. . . . Now we will have a club over them, and by God, there will be no more pampering or fiddling with them. We will do the ordering instead of going around and begging them to cooperate."[22] And because of a clause in the lease agreement, Kroc's fervid insistence on operational standards became a source of profit, too: as sales increased at a McDonald's restaurant, the rent went up, too. The owner-operator got richer, McDonald's got richer, and Americans got an honest product. Ray Kroc was a happy man.

Sonneborn, for his part, would eventually lose the faith, retiring from McDonald's as its president and selling off all his shares for a tenth of what they would later have been worth. Fred Turner, Kroc's disciple in the evangel of QSC and V, took over and guided the company to its global destiny. But Sonneborn's contribution cannot be overlooked when talking about the success of McDonald's. The hamburger was the ideal product for a hungry, prosperous, meat-eating society with a need for speed. The McDonald brothers and their space-age system created the possibility of a new industry for feeding those people, and Kroc was the perfect man to see in that industry a way to bring diverse characters together in the service of success and, in so doing, to exalt the small entrepreneurs whom he believed embodied free enterprise. But in America only the power of banks and corporate lawyers, and the immense forces they channel, will permit success on a great scale, and Sonneborn's contribution, though unlovely and colorless in every way, was as central to McDonald's as corporate capital was to America as a whole.

Thus, as with any great swath of Americana, McDonald's was the product of paradox, composed of equal parts individualism, conformity, small-scale scrabbling, immense impersonal capital, and the willingness of every diverse part and personality to move forward together, grasping for a long-hoped for and desperately desired prosperity. On the strength of a small sandwich composed of beef and bread, an economic empire was built upon which the sun never sets, one that grows larger every day—constantly receding into the horizon, necessitating infinite expansion and endless, rapacious striving. In its scale and in its soul, McDonald's truly is the Great American Success Story.

Have It Your Way

The postwar decades were the high summer of the hamburger, the years when burgers attained the summit of symbolism. The hamburger attained the status of American icon: something so often pictured, and so universally understood, that it comes to be understood by nearly everybody—a fact not wasted on Pop Artists, cartoonists, or ad men. Hamburgers by the 1960s were firmly connected with youth culture, postwar abundance, and, eventually, big business. Thus, by the late 1960s, they had come to represent much of what people liked, or didn't like, about America.

Because Ray Kroc was right. America was changing. The explosion of prosperity and modernity in the aftermath of World War II swept away much of America's decay. Some was cultural, the detritus of Victorian culture still found growing in the corners and beneath the furniture. Isolationism, some notions about race and gender, overt anti-Semitism, the belief in small government—all were swept into the air, and some years passed before they fell back down in new patterns amid the stale air. But much of the decay was physical, in the form of rotting buildings and apartments, particularly in urban centers where the Depression had suppressed new construction for many years. Developers following the lead of New York's William Levitt were discovering the attractive power of suburbs, new areas where postwar life could be writ in bright block letters on a blissfully blank slate. President Dwight Eisenhower, impressed by the efficiency of Germany's *Autobahn*, saw to it that the Federal Highway Act of 1956 was passed. The great auto companies were equally energized by new roads, greater consumer spending, and the immense expansion of the nation's infrastructure that the war had occasioned. There were more families with more people, living in new places and going to even newer ones. The hamburger, the most mobile, efficient, and satisfying sandwich ever devised, filled the vacuum at the center of all this energy expenditure. It was the perfect food to eat while driving, merrily dialing the steering wheel with one hand while holding the burger in the other, eyes firmly focused on the road to come. It was the perfect food for the atom-age family, each with its own separate sphere and interests but all united in unstated consensus; at a hamburger supper, each member of the family might eat his or her own identical meal, each with its own meat, its own starch, and its own customized condiments, all contained within easy reach of a single grasping hand. And with the enriched bun now accessible to everyone, thanks to the universal success of the hamburger, the very image of contained and mobile abundance was there for all to see.

Elisabeth Rozin, the burger's most far-seeing eulogist, writes,

> The smooth, dry, uncontaminated outer surface of the sandwich is the ideal vehicle for a handheld meal; grease, juice, stickiness, and strong food odors are kept where they belong, on the food, not the fingers. . . . Its flavor provides a suitably bland base for the savory contents; its texture is soft and pliant yet sturdy enough to stand up to a warm burger with its juicy accompaniments. Its golden brown shape, round and puffed, its promise of homespun richness, its lack of corners and hard edges, are an indication of ampleness and generosity, of unconstrained fullness. Yet nothing about the bun gets in the way of the burger itself, no crusty exterior, no yeasty bready aroma, no chewy texture. The bun as bread may not appeal to every taste; indeed, it probably does not appeal to most. But as the crucial support system of the cheeseburger, it fulfills it function admirably—pleasing everyone, offending no one.[1]

The vital center, at long last.

Because by this time the burger had, thanks to the success of McDonald's and its countless imitators, become standardized at last. The production-line hamburger, it will be remembered, got a false start at the hands of its inventors, White Castle. Today, despite that company's avid following, its hamburger is considered a niche product, a "slider" rather than a hamburger in any meaningful sense. The White Castle hamburger, by the period of postwar abundance, seemed a sad, small object, unfit for the appetite of a growing land. Not that the McDonald's hamburger was so much bigger: the fifteen-cent hamburger was never meant to be more than a sliver of beef on a bun. But the pressures of prosperity were inexorable, and by the mid-1950s, it became apparent that hamburgers, like cars, had to become bigger if they wanted to compete. The Whopper was as inevitable as the hydrogen bomb.

Thomas Hine, the cultural historian who coined the word *populuxe* to describe the aesthetic mood of the 1950s, got it right. He combined populism and luxury, adding the unnecessary "e" at the end, Madison Avenue–style, for specious prestige. Hine loves the crassness of the populuxe style, which he sees as the flowering of a long-delayed prosperity, bottled up by Victorianism, the Depression, and war. "Populuxe objects," he writes, "were symbols of achievement, affirmations that their owners had achieved a life of convenience and prosperity that their parents could only have dreamed of."[2] Populuxe means space-age designs, wild pastel color combinations, and fantastically futuristic styles laid on the most common of daily objects for the everyday consumption of average Americans living in a dream-world of material opulence. "It derives, of course, from populism and popularity . . . and it has luxury, popular luxury, luxury for all."[3]

This was the mood McDonald's capitalized on, as we have seen. But it extended to everybody with a product to sell, and the hamburger was a product that was easier and easier to sell as the 1950s took shape. The period is associated with plenty, mobility, and the rise of youth culture, and in all these things the hamburger participates as closely as ketchup with mustard. Meat had been closely rationed during the war, and in fact the removal of price controls on meat had been a hot-button issue for congressional Republicans to use against Harry Truman. (Runaway meat price inflation resulted, but nobody seemed to mind.) And it's impossible to think of youth culture in the 1950s without thinking of the drive-in as a social nexus. We've all seen it as a location for teen movies and 1950s nostalgia, but it was real, and it had an intense energy that made people want to celebrate it twenty years later. Tom Wolfe, writing about his countercultural hero Ken Kesey, does his best to convey the social life of the drive-in in all its ineffable joy.

> [Greg's Drive-In] was the high-school drive-in, with the huge streamlined sculpted pastel display sign with streaming streamlined super-slick A-22 italic script, floodlights, clamp-on trays, car-hop girls in floppy blue slacks, hamburgers in some kind of tissuey wax paper streaming with

onions pressed down and fried on the grill and mustard
and catsup to squirt all over it from out of plastic squirt
cylinders. Saturday nights when everybody is out
cruising . . . and Kesey ends up in juvenile court before
a judge and tries to tell him how it is at Greg's Drive-In
on a Saturday night: The Life—that *feeling*—The Life—
the late 1940s early 1950s American Teenage Drive-In Life
was *precisely* what it was all about—but how could you tell
anyone about it?[4]

Wolfe does his level best, and so have a hundred other less gifted
chroniclers of the American scene. Every city has its legendary
burger place, remembered fondly by middle-aged couples who
met and courted there: Dick's in Seattle, Winstead's in Kansas
City, Martin's Kum-Back in Austin. You probably had to be
there. But even without the benefit of baby-boom life experience, you can look at these drive-ins and see the energy and optimism implicit in their very architecture.

In this, too, McDonald's was an innovator. The architects
Richard McDonald hired produced dismal designs—"low, squatty
little buildings." Tilting the roof with a big overhang, though,
gave the place a forward, space-age feel. Stanley C. Meston, the
brothers' architect, accentuated Richard's design with what fast-
food design historian Philip Langdon calls "a strong, wedge-like
profile . . . [with] large windows canted upward and outward, like
those of an airport control tower." These features would all be

hallmarks of what came to be known as the Googie style, named after a coffee shop in Los Angeles. Upward sloping roofs, acute angles, starburst patterns, and other futurist imagery are its hallmarks.[5]

Googie flourished in the early 1950s because it seemed so supremely of the moment, so evocative of the better tomorrow that was right around the corner. It has become a treasure of kitsch connoisseurs who see in the Googie era's "simpler time" an ample canvas for the tracing of flattering self-portraits. But there was nothing naive about Googie; it was if nothing else worldly and self-aware, the product of the latest whiff of cutting-edge progress. Even the automotive tailfin, a laughingstock if ever there was one, was directly based on military technology: in this case, the jet fighters then struggling to break the sound barrier.

This was the part of the Cold War experience everyone remembers fondly. But there was more to the 1950s than Day-Glo design fashions and teenage kicks, even if you would never know it from the 1950s nostalgia industry. The back of the house, as they say in the restaurant business, was weaved just as tightly into the fabric of the times. "Hamburgers triumphed for still another reason," writes Jeremy Rifkin in his antibeef tirade *Beyond Beef* (1992) "—the beef industry's influence in Washington. The story of the hamburger's ascendance has as much to do with government regulation and market forces as personal taste and convenience."[6] The entire story of beef, as historians far less partisan than Rifkin have noted, is one of monopoly concentration, aided and abetted by the government. The U.S. Department of Agriculture in 1946 did an inestimable service to the beef industry, and its tireless lobby, by decreeing that hamburger could contain only beef and beef fat—that even the slightest bit of pork or pork fat disqualified it from the dignity of being called hamburger. This was a decisive blow for the beef men in the eternal war against the pork men, since it meant that they had an effective monopoly on the most popular meat product in America. Moreover, the language of the code, though foreboding, was actually loose enough, as John Love notes, "to drive a herd of cattle through."[7] Anything connected with a beef animal could be called "beef," as long as it was at least 30 percent lean. Moreover, since it was getting ground up anyway, and would be mixed with as much fat as the packer wished, it wasn't even necessary to raise beef animals for this purpose; you could just grind up worn-out dairy cows, cull animals, and beef animals that couldn't make it past even the era's highly lenient standards for palatability. It was a financial windfall and demoted pork to second-place (later third-place) status forever, despite its ancient pedigree.

Some hamburger businesses, like McDonald's, voluntarily hewed to a rigid purity code. (McDonald's is guilty of many sins, but adulterating beef has never been one of them.) Others threw in everything but the kitchen sink, and then threw the kitchen sink in, too—in the form of soy additives and other unnatural vegetable, and mineral, matter. And the meat lobbyists, on their lonely pastures miles from the nearest sheriff, had free rein to

make whatever arrangements they wished with the immense re-
tailers and food service companies to supply "hamburger" at
rock-bottom prices. Beef was now a mass commodity, tradable
profitably by only the largest producers, whose economies of
scale enabled the fast-food empires to come into being.

It's a mistake, however, to think of restaurants, front or back,
as being the engine behind the burger's rise in the 1950s. Certainly, the hamburger had an immense public place apart from
any hamburger stand or drive-in. Equally important in its history was the hamburger's home life. When not at the store feeding teenagers or going for rides with hungry motorists, the hamburger could be found on the backyard patio, sizzling away on
the home barbecue pits that had become so popular.

The backyard barbecue was a pregnant symbol in the Cold
War because it represented two powerful ideas at once. It was
first a symbol of independence. The images of Levittowns, with
their "little boxes" laid out in identical rows, evoked much scorn
at the time, and even more in the years to come, as suburban conformity began its long life as a punching bag for social critics.
But the uniformity of housing developments is what made them
cheap, and their cheapness is what made them available to nearly
everybody, particularly veterans eligible for federal mortgage
loans courtesy of the GI Bill. The American dream of home
ownership became a reality at a stroke; and if all the houses in the
new suburbs weren't available for the fantastic prices of the original Levittown, where the down payment was fifty dollars, they

were cheap enough to be in reach of most middle-class Americans. And almost all of these homes had a backyard.

There the family cookout would take place. This ritual, in which Dad, usually wearing an apron for comic effect, serves up seared meat to an adoring family, has become something of a visual trope, but it was a central part of the suburban home-ownership experience. For one thing, it was a rare opportunity for Dad to flex his muscles as provider and paterfamilias; the rest of the time, he was either a salaried functionary or, when home, deferring to Mom on all matters domestic. This made his manhood precarious, as numerous cultural historians have argued. The backyard grill was his special sphere of authority, and hamburgers were usually the star. In "Man the Barbecuer," a *New York Times* slow-day editorial opined, "Outdoor cooking, with a crowd of hungry people around, dramatizes a man to a lofty point. . . . At that moment, if nowhere else in life, the man of the house and of the fire is the complete boss."[8]

But the allure of being the Man of the House, uniting meat and fire for the eyes of the family, was only part of the appeal. There was also a crying need to make friends, to bond with neighbors, all of whom were also newcomers. The suburbanization of America set off a boom in social activities—bowling, churchgoing, women's clubs, Little League, PTAs, the Elks, and on and on. But the easiest way to socialize was to invite the neighbors over for dinner. The backyard barbecue made this festive: as *Beef Rings the Bell*, the meat-propaganda film quoted earlier, says,

In the 1950s, the iconography of backyard barbecues took on special significance, especially in light of the Cold War. Hamburgers, naturally, had a prominent place.

even the process of broiling the hamburgers is fun and promotes friendship and good fellowship.

The social aspect of home barbecuing was one reason the fad had legs. The other was America's new place in the world. A funny thing happened on the way to the future: the United States, a country on the brink of dissolution from scarcity, woke up the day after World War II and found itself the only rich nation in a poor world. What's more, it was rich even by American standards: nobody could get over how plush life had gotten once the initial Truman-era transition to a peacetime economy had taken place. The baby boom happened because times were good—the American economy had come out of the Depression, buoyed up by massive government spending, newfound stability in the world market, and the fact that every country this side of Russia needed to buy our products or raw materials and—thanks to the wisdom of the Marshall Plan—had money to do so. American exceptionalism was never more justified than in these years, when kids were told to eat their food "because children were starving in China." They were, too; and it suited the American mind to suppose that America was well fed, well clothed, and well housed, to paraphrase President Franklin D. Roosevelt. Later, there would be dissent about this, and President John F. Kennedy would begin remedial measures. But if there was one thing the average American could agree on, it was that we were, in the words of historian David Potter, a "people of plenty."[9] And how better to demonstrate that prosperity than a ceremonial meat-feed? The postwar meat shortage had been no joke; most Americans took it for granted that meat, and only meat, sufficed to make the body healthy, and there had not been enough to go around for a long time. Even before the Depression, Herbert Hoover had spoken of "a chicken in every pot" as a utopian ideal. Meat was rationed in World War II and afterward was subject

Have It Your Way

first to wild inflation and then to a dramatic shortage in the fall of 1946.[10] Now, in the first flush times many Americans could remember, there was all the meat you could want. And it just so happened that the rest of the world was either devastated by war or living under the iron heel of communism.

The American love of meat, particularly in its cheapest, most accessible form, was thus also a rebuke to the Reds. The hamburger was a nonpareil icon of easy abundance, and a loaded one at that, when pointed at the lands behind the Iron Curtain, where people (it was imagined) had to survive on gray porridge and they could shoot you for laughing in bed. One of the period's most publicized confrontations was the famous "kitchen debate" between Vice President Nixon and Soviet premier Nikita Khrushchev at the American National Exhibition in Moscow in 1959. Nixon's position was that our superiority to the Russians was a result not of missiles or bombs but rather of the awe-inspiring comfort and abundance of the American home.

Cold War liberals frequently made the same claim in explicitly political forums, but more often it showed up in popular culture in the form of newspaper stories either celebrating the conquest of foreign nations by the hamburger ("What Iran needs most is not only western technologies but also such edibles as hamburgers") or celebrating our own meatitude ("Beef Eating at an All-Time High in U.S.").[11]

Hamburgers, humble yet bountiful, made perfect propaganda—a fact not wasted on advertisers, who pictured them frequently in ads for everything from soda to scouring pads. Rarely was the hamburger the focus of the ad, as in the "food porn" created by food stylists in later years. More frequently, the burger was incidental, a part of the Great American Eating experience. This would be a hallmark of burger propaganda for years to come. And there would need to be a lot of propaganda, because as the baby boom flooded the country with hungry, prosperous young families, it became apparent to anyone who had eyes in their head that there was money to be made in the hamburger business. McDonald's, having invented the industry, for a few brief years had the field largely to itself; but as the brothers had learned in their San Bernardino operation, the rudiments of the way they did business, at least in the kitchen, were easily copied. In the 1960s, American roads and GI systems were subject to a flood of Burger Chefs, Burger Tymes, Burger Backyards, Burger Queens, Sonics, Hardee's, Big Boys, Steak and Shakes, A&Ws, and Royal Castles.

One of the most successful early rivals of McDonald's, though, was one of the few that actually differed from McDonald's in a fundamental way. Insta-Burger King, later shortened to Burger King, was by far the most formidable of its many rivals and the only one that ever seriously challenged it for the affection of the American public. The chain was hamstrung by bad management; after its purchase in 1967 by the Pillsbury Company, it had one corporate owner after another and was consigned to ongoing neglect. Even so, it alone of all the hamburger chains that flourished like wildflowers in the fertility of 1950s America rose up and stood against McDonald's. It did this, I think, because it came almost as close to McDonald's did to the wellsprings of the century's business energy. Its founders, James McLamore and David Edgerton, were every bit as grandiose in their ambitions as Ray Kroc; they just happened to stumble across the McDonald brothers' San Bernardino operation after Kroc did. And of course, they made the fatal mistake of "merging," or rather selling, to a company they did not control and that had no abiding interest in hamburgers. But as hamburger men, the two rode the trade winds on the same wings as Kroc.

McDonald's signal invention, it will be remembered, was neither the hamburger nor the franchise (although certainly Harry Sonneborn's magic was inventive). Rather, it was the production line method of making hamburgers and thus delivering them up to a stream of customers waiting with Pavlovian desire to exchange their money for a predictable meal. Burger King went McDonald's one better. The chain had begun life in a Miami suburb in 1954 as Insta-Burger King and featured the world's first totally automated hamburger. The Insta-Burger was the product of a classic American machine fetish, the precise gastronomical equivalent of the conveyor belts and burnished rollers that figured so prominently in the educational films and newsreels of the time. Truly, the Insta-Burger was the Hamburger of the Future. It passed, along with its bun, on chain-borne conveyers through a complex system of heating elements, along with its bun, until both were delivered to the point of service operative at precisely the same moment. There was no NASA-like precision to this operation in practice; it was infinitely less efficient in the long run than a guy standing there flipping burgers next to a lazy Susan. But the idea of it! The promotional literature advanced to potential franchisees boasted that the Insta-Burger could cook four hundred burgers and buns an hour.

In fact, the Insta-Burger was "a rube goldberg device," as Jim McLamore called it.[12] Soon after taking over, McLamore re-designed the process, creating the horizontal broiler conveyor belt still in service today. The system was patented and the "Insta-" dropped forever. The broiled burger was said to taste better than the traditional griddled variety and fed into the national cookout craze. (Some Burger Kings even had "backyard patios" built into them.)

And then in 1957 McLamore added his own flourish to the newly launched business. He noticed that people liked a big hamburger they were eating at a rival restaurant. The reason they liked it, he gathered, was because it was big. So, he reasoned, why not make a big hamburger at Burger King? But he needed a name that was big. "I suggested that we call our product a *Whopper*, knowing that this would convey imagery of something *big*," he explains thoughtfully in his autobiography, *The Burger King*.[13] Amazingly, Burger King would have the field to itself for almost twenty years, since the imperious McDonald's did not fire back until 1972 with the invention of the Quarter Pounder. (The original jumbo burger, the Big Boy, would make it to a national stage only in 1968 as the Big Mac, the victim of ad hoc franchising and the lack of an empire-building vision.)

Big hamburgers were an innovation so obvious that you have to wonder what the holdup was. Everything was growing in the 1950s: cars, families, the population, the economy. But really, a big hamburger had much built-in ideology working against it. The whole concept of the hamburger business was based on cheap, tiny, tasty objects that cost almost nothing to make and could be sold for not much more. At a time when the standard was a fifteen-cent burger, or at most one costing eighteen cents, the Whopper cost a whopping twenty-nine. It seemed totally against the spirit of the burger business to make a sandwich that had a 44 percent food cost, as the Whopper did. You had to charge a lot more for a sandwich like that, which meant you would sell less of them, which meant less profit. This was how you were going to compete with McDonald's? But Burger King found out what the whole fast-food industry would come to learn: Americans like bigger products and are willing to pay for them. Burger King sold more Whoppers than anything else. By 1967, it was building a hundred new restaurants a year, equaling McDonald's pace—an unheard-of feat, albeit one that didn't last long.

And still other companies flourished. Burger Chef was more aggressive than Burger King and even more innovative. The company invented the value meal combo of soda, fries, and burger for one price; it was the first to give away a toy with the meal. Burger Chef had broiled hamburgers and an automated conveyor-belt system, and it was the first to pioneer the movie tie-in, in the twilight of its existence, when Burger Chef did a cross-promotion with *Star Wars* in 1977. But all the burger chains met the same fate, swallowed up by vast and indifferent corporations. Pillsbury bought Burger King in 1967. General Foods bought Burger Chef the same year. In 1968 Ralston Purina acquired Jack in the Box, a major regional chain in California, and made it a national brand. Every one, reduced to a division of an immense and unwieldy corporation, and supervised by managers with neither interest nor experience in the hamburger business, was either destroyed or crippled. Only McDonald's escaped the holocaust. Consolidated Foods was prepared to make McDonald's a princely offer, but Ray Kroc hadn't slaved to make his life's work a column in some other company's annual report. "You've got a marvelous company, and [the offer] is a great compliment," Kroc told Nate Cummings, Consolidated's domineering CEO. "The problem is that we just wouldn't consider something like that unless we were the surviving company, and I'm afraid that managing a company like yours is just more than we could handle."[14] The meeting ended, and McDonald's turned to conquering the future with renewed energy and a flattened field of competition.

All the same, it was a sad bit of business. The primacy of McDonald's in the years that followed has been a cause more often of regret than for triumph, except perhaps for McDonald's stockholders. The corporatization of the burger industry is not a pretty story and makes a tedious tale even for business students. Cutthroat competition between starry-eyed hamburger men, each one reaching for the Next Big Thing, is far more in keeping with the ideals of American culture. But by the 1960s, it was obvious to all concerned that the days of rugged independence were long gone. You didn't need Frederick Jackson Turner to tell you that the frontier was closed off or a weatherman to tell you how the wind blew. The antiestablishment impulse that would seem so widespread among the young in the 1960s didn't really express itself in foodways. Although a few radicalized parties might have taken up brown bread, the baby boomers were largely suburban, and few had the stomach to give up thick hamburgers, cold glasses of whole milk, burnished roast turkeys, and all the other treasures and fetishes of American middle-class life. What came into disrepute instead was the whole money-grubbing, mass-marketed, artificial enterprise that was big business in general. Fast food was one of the tawdriest and most visible manifestations of that, as well as one the boomers knew intimately well. This was not the highly developed case against mass consumption and its discontents articulated by John Kenneth Galbraith in *The Affluent Society* or Tom Hayden in the Port Huron Statement; this was rather a mood that expressed itself in a hundred ways.

Consider a comic strip from *Zap Comix* #2. The comic, published in San Francisco in 1968 by Charles Plymell, the housemate of Jack Kerouac and Allen Ginsberg, was a showcase for

Robert Crumb, the best known and most influential of the "underground comix" artists of the period. (Art critic Robert Hughes has called Crumb "the one and only genius the 1960s underground produced in visual art, either in America or Europe.")[15] One of Crumb's special gifts was his bone-deep sense of American popular culture, and a lot of his early work, such as in *Zap*, parodies mainstream culture of the 1950s. (Hippies are scarcely anywhere in Crumb.) In "Hamburger Hi-Jinx," an ebullient businessman exclaims his love for hamburgers. Heading toward a big, ultramodern-looking burger palace in one of Crumb's stylized cityscapes, he tells us, "You know what I want? You know what I need? You know what I'm getting?"

The buildup continues until the next page. The grill man, another high-spirited all-American type, serves him up the burger, and the two are so enamored of it that they spend an entire page just admiring it. Cheesis K. Reist, the hero, is about to consummate the relationship when the tale turns trippy: the anthropomorphic burger, ketchup, and mustard warn him of impending karmic doom.

Naturally, like any red-blooded American, he pays no heed, devouring the burger in an orgy of block-letter sound effects: "Haw haw, munch, glom, choff, gulp, glumpf," with expressive droplets of food flying in every direction. But the burger's warning comes true right away. Cheesis smashes the talking bottles and leaves the burger joint but is immediately tripped by toughs and run over by noisy trucks. A broken man, shoeless and in tatters, he sits forlorn on a curb, cursing his fate, until he realizes what can make him whole again: "Another hamburger!"

"Hamburger Hi-Jinx" is an early expression of the progressive mood of the time. America had been so recklessly ravenous and hedonistic for so long—wouldn't we ever have to pay the piper? Would not hubris eventually be served? *The Whole Earth Catalog*, in many ways the moral center of the countercultural movement, reminded its readers: "Everything's connected to everything. / Everything's got to go somewhere. / There's no such thing as a free lunch."[16] Eventually, this perspective would take up permanent residence in its own corner of America in the form of the environmental movement. But Crumb was no philosopher. He hated hippies as much as he hated squares. It was in his effortlessly parodic style that he represented the future. Crumb's art was in the vanguard of a new sensibility in America, a knowing, referential perspective that took American iconography for granted. It could be found everywhere from the 1960s onward, fully formed and mocking affectionately as only a tradition's natural inheritors are wont to do. At first, it came across as merely arch, an exaggerated and stylized art of the kind Susan Sontag wrote about in 1964's "Notes on 'Camp.'" The over-the-top style of ABC's *Batman* series was one manifestation of this. But Sontag's essay registered precisely because she was putting a name to something that was in the air. "Camp sees everything in quotation marks," she wrote.[17] And hamburgers were one of those things in quotation marks.

Just ask Andy Warhol. When *Time* discovered pop art in 1963, it was Warhol to whom the magazine pointed: "Even Manhattan's Museum of Modern Art has bought a pop art sculpture called Dual Hamburger," it marveled. To *Time*, the act of celebrating something as lowly and universal as the hamburger was the proof of pop art's ultracool irony: "Hamburger is an admirable choice; it embodies all the values of pop art—which is essentially a mild, unrebellious comment on the commonplace made by picturing it without any pretense of taste or orthodox technical skill."[18] Like the other pop artists, Warhol's art existed entirely in a spectatorial space; the artist, and by invitation the viewer, was put at an Olympian remove from everyday objects. Not natural objects, mind you—a pool of Warhol water lilies or plate of apples wouldn't make any sense. The idea was to take man-made objects that existed as units of social meaning and redirect them. That was Warhol's special gift, but the other pop artists participated in more or less the same way.

Claes Oldenburg, a Swede, took the project to titanic proportions. As a foreigner in America, Oldenburg had by birth the outsider's perspective that was pop art's reason for being; he was known for his immense, outsized sculpture of everyday objects and objects made of soft, puffy fabrics. Thus, 1962's *Floor Burger.*

Oldenburg's objects are intended to be instantly recognizable; what's remarkable about *Floor Burger* is how identifiable it is. (*Soft Toilet* and *Soft Bathtub* are nearly unrecognizable, like the

The hamburger as ironic referent arrived with pop art: *top*, Andy Warhol's
Hamburger (1985–1986) . . . and, *bottom*, Claes Oldenburg's *Floor Burger* (1962).

limp hides of skinned animals.) Perhaps the artist couldn't bring himself to distort the image too much. "I create forms from a living situation: a hamburger is something a living form would create," he told *Time*.[19] For the next forty years, the hamburger would serve artists well, registering as a symbol of carnal, corrupt mass culture (as in Mel Ramos's 1965 *Virnaburger*) or merely as a pop-cultural punch line (as in David LaChapelle's 2002 *Death from a Hamburger*).

There was a price to pay for becoming an American institution. In one way or another, all the burger chains paid it. The American consumer paid it, too, once the novelty of hamburgers had worn off and burgers had become a popular but unexciting part of the national diet, a mainstay every bit as boring and banal as hash. By the 1960s, White Castle, the Hamburger Adam, was reduced to a niche product in urban areas, set apart from the boundless green plains that were the suburbs. Only 112 were open in 1970s, catering largely to the same urban, all-male, working-class clientele as always. And White Castle couldn't expand, because Billy Ingram was famously committed to standards of control, both operational and financial, that prevented the company from enjoying the corporate gold rush of the 1960s. The last of the great industrialists, Ingram went to his grave in 1966 knowing that White Castle, though profitable, was a weak sister in the industry it had created. These were sad years for

White Castle. There was even talk high within the company of creating a soy burger. A soy burger! Could there be a grosser violation of the whole enterprise? An even sadder moment, perhaps the nadir of the White Castle saga, occurred when Edgar Ingram, the company's hereditary chieftain, recommissioned the famous University of Minnesota study to see if man could live by burgers alone. This time, the results were negative. "Although we would not want to advertise that a person could live on White Castle products alone, we will have the satisfaction of knowing we are doing a good job," wrote Ingram, wistfully.[20]

It was the same in the suburbs. The way America ate had changed; restaurant food was a part of daily life now, at every level of society. The controlling intelligences at Pillsbury, Ralston Purina, and the other food conglomerates cast their lot with the chains, and over the next few years Kentucky Fried Chicken, Hardee's, Pizza Hut, Taco Bell, Arby's, and nearly every other chain went down the corporate maw. In the end only White Castle and McDonald's, fittingly, were left standing.

McDonald's was not left unscathed. Kroc lived into the 1970s but turned control of the corporation over to his protégé Fred Turner, a hamburger man's hamburger man, the guy who literally wrote the book on operations. But McDonald's had drifted from its hamburger mission anyway. There was no resisting the zeitgeist. McDonald's expanded at a breakneck pace through the 1960s and 1970s, but only through the departures from the company's original purpose and mission. The menu expanded, prices rose, and the company began to take on the character, not of a spunky underdog, but of a voracious and overreaching overlord, a U.S. Steel of the burger business. It imposed corporate conformity on the nation, or so it was said. "Customers get almost as little discretion as the help; their burgers come wrapped, with ketchup and mustard applied in precise, premeasured splats. A rugged individualist can order his burger 'without,' but he will have to discover that concession on his own. . . . McDonald's manages to make its licensees, restaurant managers and burger slingers seem as standardized as its machines and cuisine," wrote a disillusioned *Time* magazine.[21] The company's once-stainless public relations took a beating, too, when Kroc gave a massive contribution to President Nixon's reelection fund, a fact for which he would have taken much Watergate-era heat anyway. But at the time, the federal government was attempting to control inflation through a complicated price-control bureaucracy, and when Kroc wanted to raise the price of the new Quarter Pounder to pay for a much-needed second slice of cheese, he had to go before the Wage and Price Control Board, which approved it. Washington observers, seeing Trickiness everywhere, saw a quid pro quo between the contribution and the approval, not to mention the ongoing question of a minimum wage increase, which Kroc was naturally opposed to. McDonald's was now the establishment and had to take its lumps. When it opened one of its first New York City stores, on the Upper East Side, a coalition of bluebloods protested, condemning McDonald's as the embodiment of everything bad about mainstream America. The *New York Times Magazine* wrote a cover story on "The Burger That's Eating New York," and a *Barron's* article by a CUNY accounting professor accused the company of financial improprieties. Even children's television moguls Sid and Marty Krofft got their licks in on McDonald's when the two sued over the resemblance of McDonaldland characters to the felt-covered cast of the Kroffts' children's show *H.R. Pufnstuf.* McDonald's lost this battle, but not before being reduced to arguing that Pufnstuf wore a cummerbund where Mayor McCheese, his McDonaldland doppelgänger, sported a diplomat's sash. The judge, unmoved, ruled for the Kroffts.

Meanwhile, Americans ate more hamburgers than ever and felt worse about it. Burger chains went in and out of business. Meat prices continued to increase, along with everything else. The promise of the baby boom and JFK's New Frontier seemed to have ended with Watergate, Vietnam, and inflation, and with it went the standard-bearing symbols of postwar culture. The hamburger was no more a sign of plenty and enjoyment, despite constant growth and greater hype. America was in a malaise, all right. *The Whole Earth Catalog* had it right in its dire warning:

Everything's connected to everything.
Everything's got to go somewhere.
There's no such thing as a free lunch.

The Hamburger in Power

"My first car was a '54 Ford," begins one review of George Lucas's 1973 film *American Graffiti*. "When I went to see George Lucas's 'American Graffiti' that whole world—a world that now seems incomparably distant and innocent—was brought back with a rush of feeling that wasn't so much nostalgia as culture shock. Remembering my high school generation, I can only wonder at how unprepared we were for the loss of innocence that took place in America with the series of hammer blows beginning with the assassination of President Kennedy."[1] The critic, Roger Ebert, was thirty-one years old. Though not technically a baby boomer, he spoke for the generation then coming into its prime in America. Having been children in the 1950s and teenagers or young adults in the 1960s, these young Americans naturally perceived the years of their childhood as "an innocent time," a Presleyan paradise of hot rods, sock hops, and unironic television shows. The cult of the 1950s emerged full-blown in the early 1970s, with *Grease*, Sha Na Na, the rediscovery of Buddy Holly, and so on.[2] This vision of a semi-mindless, "innocent" 1950s imposed by the baby boom on American culture has yet to be effaced: only show a pipe-smoking father or a boy in a varsity sweater, and any American can recite the era's misremembered clichés chapter and verse. We know the 1950s the way that Maimonides knew the Talmud. It started with *American Graffiti*.

And at the center of *American Graffiti* is a hamburger stand.

There was a certain justice to this. The baby boomers weren't wrong to think of themselves as having lived in their own sealed-off pleasure dome. They came of age in a period of unprecedented security and prosperity, and an entire culture sprang up around them, its growth sped and swollen by technology and spending power. There were transistors for little cheap radios and cathode tubes for television so they could have their own mass media. Even the record player became portable, a cheap fold-up appliance a kid could keep in the bedroom. And there were lots of cheap cars and lots of cheap gas, and lots of jobs that anybody could get and do. About the only thing that American teenagers in the 1950s lacked, in terms of lifestyle, was a public space they could call their own. And as often as not this took the form of a drive-in restaurant like Mel's, the center of *American Graffiti*.

The original Mel's Drive-In was a northern California institution, the first of the L.A. drive-ins successfully copied to San

Francisco. (Every California town's youth culture would largely center around the drive-in. Ken Kesey's, in Portland, Oregon, revolved around Greg's; two generations of Seattleites met at Dick's.) George Lucas, growing up in northern California, naturally thought of it when conceiving of a social locus for *American Graffiti*. One thing that had brought the Woodstock Nation into being, after all, was the singular condition of its members having had their own cars, restaurants, jobs, and disposable incomes.

American Graffiti struck a chord; costing a mere $777,000 to make, it took in over $21 million and was nominated for two Academy Awards—Best Picture and, for Lucas, Best Director. More important, in establishing 1950s nostalgia at a stroke, it set the template for an entire growth industry in the 1970s. *Graffiti* star Ron Howard, himself a 1950s television icon, became the medium's face of the 1950s: an episode of *Love, American Style* called "Love and the Happy Day" featured Howard as an all-American teen and actress Marion Ross as Howard's Donna Reed–esque mother. The response was so positive, particularly among children who knew of the 1950s only what they saw on television, that a series was greenlighted to star Howard and Ross. It was pointedly named *Happy Days* and became, in a major zeitgeist shift, the most popular show on television since Norman Lear's politically charged *All in the Family*. *Happy Days* was about as political as its title suggested; it centered around a hamburger drive-in restaurant owned by Arnold, played by the Nisei actor Pat Morita. Later, a spin-off starring Howard's *American*

Graffiti co-star Cindy Williams displaced *Happy Days* as the country's number-one show. The hamburger was now an unmistakable symbol of American innocence. "Burgers and fries and cherry pies, it was simple and good back then," went the chorus of a major 1978 hit for Charley Pride. And the hamburger chains did everything in the power to leverage that feeling.

At its core, though, hamburger nostalgia was a lucrative lie. The hamburger, it was forgotten, hadn't become the official fast food of America until the 1960s. Like *American Graffiti* itself, it was a product of that decade and of the vast powers of capital investment the postwar boom had made available for marginal pursuits like fast food or art movies. The universality of burgers in the Kennedy and Johnson years was purely a product of aggressive expansion, easy money, and cutting-edge food service technology and management. Insofar as the 1950s nostalgia boom positioned the hamburger as the great American food, it misled. The primacy of hamburgers in the American diet was a product of the hamburger's years of corporate ascendancy more than anything else. Hamburgers were a corporate entity every bit as much as plastics or television; essentially, they represented the secret life of the 1960s intruding on the 1970s in the form of the 1950s. But as long as kids kept watching *Happy Days* and eating at McDonald's, no one pressed the issue too closely.

Well, almost no one. By the 1970s, the New Left and the counterculture had come and gone, leaving behind American progressive ideology in more or less its modern form. Simply put, this amounted to an opposition energy activated by the Vietnam War and the Nixon administration. The "movement" having more or less petered out with the war's end and Nixon's triumphant (as was thought) reelection, leftism during the 1970s was more a cultural movement than a political one, as was frequently noted. The polarizing energies of the White House were perfectly configured to bring it into being: Nixon had ridden into power on the loathings of the Silent Majority, and the lines appeared to be pretty well drawn. In hating Nixon, big business, the war, and the middle-class mores that Nixon claimed as his reason for being, leftists in the 1970s were taking the only course available to them. Necessarily, that meant hating hamburgers and the hegemony they represented. Leftism had been bequeathed a crypto-Hindu, green streak anyway; the place of the hamburger as a platform for low wages, a commodity wielded by corporate power, and, worst of all, a weapon of cultural imperialism, earned it a special place of dishonor. There were armed hamburger standoffs in Cleveland and Detroit. But the most dramatic political hamburger battle of all was being fought in the Far East.

Yes, it was true: having failed to win the hearts and minds of Asia by brute force, America was now trying to do it through the McDonald's bacillus. A war against the global expansion of McDonald's began and has been waged, without success, up until the present time. The image of McDonald's hamburgers, marching in lockstep in endless phalanxes, conquering the world for the forces of homogeneity, has haunted nationalists around the world for thirty years. It was certainly not encouraged by the company's first foray into Asia in the 1970s. With the same fearsomely focused imitativeness with which they were proceeding to lick us at the auto business, Japan was preparing to plunge into the burger program. The Japanese entrepreneur behind the enterprise, Den Fujita, went out of his way to put it in the most pugnacious and incendiary way possible: "The reason Japanese people are so short and have yellow skins," he opined, "is because they have eaten nothing but fish and rice for two thousand years. If we eat McDonald's hamburgers and potatoes for a thousand years we will become taller, our skin will become white, and our hair blond."[3] In my college library copy of John Love's *McDonald's: Behind the Arches*, this quotation is underlined and marked for special emphasis with a five-pointed star. "AMERICANIZATION" is written emphatically in the margin.

And there were other people, too, with an objection to the hamburger status quo. Dave Thomas, an early protégé of Colonel Sanders, had made his bones in the fast-food business and, after rescuing four failing Columbus, Ohio, Kentucky Fried Chicken franchises and becoming a millionaire in the process, set his sights on the industry's ultimate prize: a hamburger business to rival McDonald's.

It wasn't an auspicious hour. After the great corporate shakeout, the market was saturated with immense, moribund hamburger chains, many of which were underperforming conspicuously. Wall Street, on which the hamburger macroeconomy finally rested, was less than impressed with the business as a whole. A recession was thought, correctly, to be looming around the corner. And Columbus had no shortage of hamburgers. There were McDonald's and Burger Kings all over the place, and the city also happened to be the home base of White Castle. All of this impressed Thomas not at all. He was brother to dragons, the last of the great burger tycoons, the Teddy Roosevelt of the Hamburger Mount Rushmore. (Walter Anderson and Billy Ingram can be imagined to Thomas's right; Ray Kroc, leftward, in the Lincoln position.)

Thomas is known remembered affectionately today for his down-to-earth persona on Wendy's TV commercials. Taking a page from the Colonel's book, he personified the values with which Wendy's sought to be associated: old-fashioned character, value, and quality such as was imagined to have preceded the fast-food era. And in fact, Wendy's was founded on the central insight that handsome profits might be made from charging more for a better, larger hamburger, freshly made and composed to the customer's specifications. Wendy's made hamburgers with corners that stuck outside the bun, a simple trick that simultaneously conveyed size (the standard burger was as big as a Whopper), homey nonconformity (it didn't fit the bun), and plenty (there was literally more there than the bun could contain). More important, each burger was cooked to order from fresh beef, a service that had become obsolete as the burger business had industrialized itself. The Wendy's burger cost fifty-five cents when McDonald's was still selling an eighteen-cent hamburger but was so manifestly bigger and better that sales boomed. And most amazingly, at a time when a quarter-pound hamburger was hyperbolically touted as a Whopper, an object so immense that only a titan's appetite could suffice to consume it, Wendy's quietly made available half-pound and even three-quarter-pound burgers, albeit with the same single slice of cheese. Wendy's stressed its preindustrial integrity over and over, most visibly through an "old-fashioned" motif featuring turn-of-the-century catalog advertisements and a logo presenting a wholesome freckled girl with braided hair and a cameo.

But there was another side to Thomas as well. Though he completely believed in his primary product and the old-timey rigmarole that surrounded it, he was an incisive, hyperefficient restaurant professional conditioned to the most extreme conditions of competition. Though the hamburger business had been based on car culture, had started out with drive-ins, most operations had done away with drive-in service, a huge hassle that invited all kinds of juvenile delinquents in search of sexcapades. There were more cars than ever on the roads, though, and Thomas steered them to Wendy's by inventing the drive-through window. Now he could sell more hamburgers to more people with less space and less capital. And though Wendy's was designed to summon the mood of a more welcoming, slower time, it was in fact geared to maximum speed: Thomas designed the first flow architecture aimed at getting consumers into one door and out the other with minimal loitering. Even the seats were deliberately made uncomfortable to discourage lingering. Later, Wendy's would be among the first chains to diversify its menu successfully, adding salads and baked potatoes for health-conscious Americans and eventually pulling into a dead heat with Burger King as the number-two hamburger in America. By 1972, it was already an unqualified success. From a single Columbus restaurant three years earlier, the chain had multiplied by nine and was earning almost two million dollars a year.

Neither Burger King nor McDonald's was about to take Wendy's lying down. As the upstart chain grew increasingly successful throughout the 1970s, both chains counterattacked. McDonald's brought out the Quarter Pounder in 1972; Burger King brought out its "Have it your way" campaign in 1974. Still Wendy's continued to grow. Eventually, the public would be treated to an all-out "burger war" in which each of the three chains would explicitly attack the other two on television commercials. The best-remembered moment of the episode is surely Walter Mondale's alluding to a Wendy's commercial during a debate with his Democratic primary opponent Gary Hart; but that tame bit of political theater, like the "Where's the beef?" catchphrase upon which it took its short and stunted flight, mattered less than the three-way gridlock of the burger wars. Hamburgers, in the 1970s, had become like so much else in postwar American culture: a huge business, but tawdry and depressing. The teenager's frisky Mustang was now the harried housewife's Pinto, a.. the fact that Ford was still a huge company did little for consumer morale. The hamburger wars were part of what fast-food industry analyst Robert Emerson called "the endless shakeout" of that business. Chains bloomed and withered or were bought out by corporate parents. Commercial campaigns came and went and were forgotten. Burgers were part of America, and America was in a malaise. Those inside the industry had known this for ten years, but it now became depressingly apparent to the culture as a whole.

Meanwhile, the stasis of the Burger Trust notwithstanding, fast food in America continued to grow, like the ecosystems that spring up around the feet of immense trees in old-growth forests. American consumer taste was famously volatile anyway, and as the baby boomers aged, they naturally looked to new food "concepts" to feed themselves and their families. "The population is maturing," noted a 1986 article in *Restaurant Business*, "both in age and in level of sophistication, and as eating out becomes an accepted part of American life, consumers are seeking diversity in their dining experiences." This translated to the rise, in the early and mid-1980s, of Taco Bell, Domino's, Quik Wok, Arby's, Long John Silver's, Subway, and untold other chains, all existing alongside the burger giants. Was this then the wave of the future, the natural inheritance of a polyglot America? Would not fast food become, like the nation it served, a "melting pot" of ethnic concepts? "Nowadays, ethnic food is getting to be nearly as

much in demand as hamburgers, leading some observers to wonder if it isn't just a matter of time before squid in *nam pla* sauce
becomes the finger food of the moment."[4]

Well, *that* never happened. And neither were hamburgers on
the run. But as a symbol of the establishment, in the 1970s and
afterward, they were prone to the assaults of all comers. The
realm where this was felt most was, naturally, in the area of their
greatest power, the great fast-food empires. But so, too, were
hamburgers vulnerable to criticism and scorn socially and intel-
lectually. Everyone could take for granted that hamburger places
were low, cheesy, and déclassé; that went without saying. But the
leftist critique of the hamburger, which had been gestating since
the 1960s, had by the 1980s become entrenched in the academy.
While "popular culture" studies had started in the 1970s with a
loose, egalitarian mission in small liberal arts colleges like Bowling Green in Ohio, by the 1980s, the study of American culture
had become a major academic industry. With an ideology and
vocabulary borrowed from a century of avant-garde European
intellectuals, the culture studies industry was oriented toward a
progressive critique of social norms. To generalize in the loosest
possible way, it opposed the status quo, particularly regarding
the consumer society and the corporate oligarchy that supported
it. To borrow a word from one of its great influences, the Marxist
philosopher Antonio Gramsci, they saw in the dominion of the
great American sandwich a form of hegemony—or, rather, ham-
burgemony.

The essence of this critique, which did no economic harm to the hamburger bushiness but which was as easily absorbed by American college graduates as beef juice by a bun, was twofold. There was an environmental side, which held out that beef was bad for the health of the human race and the environment, for a number of well-evidenced reasons; and there was a social critique, which held that hamburgers were a medium for exploitation—of workers, of consumers, of children. Both sides of the critique have been articulated forcefully in recent years: by Eric Schlosser in his influential book *Fast Food Nation* and by documentarian Morgan Spurlock in his film *Super Size Me*, in which the filmmaker ate nothing but McDonald's meals for thirty days, to near-catastrophic effect. "[There] lies a simple explanation for why eating a hamburger can now make you seriously ill," Schlosser wrote of "the national dish." "There is shit in the meat."[5]

Though the most visible and successful of recent attacks on the hamburger, Schlosser's and Spurlock's attacks were both aimed largely at the fast-food business. And yet there was much said against hamburgers themselves, particularly by serious environmentalists. Their larger claims, such as the hubris implicit in our belief that we can and should eat everything all the time, has yet to gain traction in America. But some of their scientific arguments—for example, that the clearing of forests to create grazing pastures in the Third World is contributing to world desertification and the greenhouse effect—are hard to dismiss and gain force with each passing year. In *Beyond Beef*, environmentalist Jeremy Rifkin writes of cows as "hooved locusts" that are literally consuming the planet:

> The ever-increasing cattle population is wreaking havoc on the earth's ecosystems, destroying habitats on six continents. Cattle raising is a primary factor in the destruction of the world's remaining tropical rain forests. . . . The overgrazing of semiarid and arid lands has left parched and barren deserts on four continents. Organic runoff from feedlots is now a major source of organic pollution in our nation's groundwater. Cattle are also a major cause of global warming. . . . They consume over 70 percent of all the grain produced in the United States. . . . While millions of human beings go hungry for lack of adequate grain, millions more in the industrial word die from diseases caused by an excess of grain-fed animal flesh, and especially beef, in their diets.[6]

Few critics see beef production in such apocalyptic terms. But all agree that the sustaining infrastructure of the hamburger business was at best a problem and at worst a disgrace. The desertification Rifkin refers to is a result largely of the needs of the hamburger business. The cows that are eating up the vegetation of South America are lean, gnarly creatures that never see the soft light of a steakhouse or the happy gaze of a family surrounding a roast beef. They get made into hamburger. Without cheap range-fed beef from South America, the American beef industry would collapse. In this sense, the critics have a strong Marxist argument built right into the hamburger infrastructure. "American beef consumption continues to rest upon the availability of grassland . . . [opened up by] a process of international capitalist underdevelopment in which arable land is actually being converted to cattle pasture and being withdrawn from local subsistence production," writes cultural materialist Eric B. Ross.[7] Nor was that all. Anyone who has a problem with the beef industry in America by necessity has a problem with hamburgers. Hamburger production was, and is, the gasoline that makes the whole engine run. Dairy cows, once used up, can be sold for hamburger; that keeps the price of milk down. The discarded fat from feedlot cows is what allows grass-fed foreign beef to taste good as hamburgers; profit from this waste product helps keep the price of beef down. ("The union of feedlot fat with range-fed lean beef takes place in the industrial grinders from which they emerge transubstantiated into the nation's supply of hamburger meat," writes Marvin Harris, poetically.)[8] Thanks to an infinite appetite for the world's most popular sandwich, the hamburger covers a multitude of sins.

Environmentalists had a legitimate beef with the hamburger, so to speak. But it was the hamburger's social life that inspired the greatest fury and the greatest fallout. Although the fast-food industry as a whole was proverbially oppressive, one company in particular came to represent its ills everywhere. McDonald's, to the world (and to a sector of the American public), represented everything bad about America. Part of this was merely aesthetic; more often, though it was nationalistic. The golden arches were an advancing infantry wedge, marching mercilessly over native culture and workers' rights.

The hamburger reached its apotheosis when, if a market report quoted by Eric Schlosser is to be believed, the McDonald's logo became "more widely recognized than the Christian cross."[9] The *New York Times* summed up McDonald's globewide troubles in 2003: "In Quito, Ecuador, protestors burned a Ronald McDonald statue. In Paris, demonstrators smashed a McDonald's window. South Korean activists calling for an end to the war sought attention by scaling a McDonald's sign. Other McDonald's outlets—in Karachi, in Buenos Aires—have been ringed with police officers to stave off trouble."[10]

Which is not to say that McDonald's failed in any of these countries. How could it? Its power source was the harnessed fusion energy of local entrepreneurs and omnipotent corporate power. It was the core of the American sun, at least as far as capitalism was concerned. Though American-style "free trade" didn't have quite as good a name in the 1980s and 1990s as it did in the 1950s, it was incalculably more powerful: a year after the fall of communism, the world's busiest McDonald's was operating in Moscow's Pushkin Square.

The hamburger, for all its tarnish, was in fact the most powerful food object in the industrialized world. And after two decades spent in the shadows of controversy and the blinding glare of profit, the hamburger emerged at the turn of new millennium ready to take back its rightful position at the top of the food chain.

The Haute Burger Skirmish of 2003 will go down, no doubt, as one of those freakish episodes that occasionally enliven restaurant history: Daniel Boulud going hammer-and-tongs with the Old Homestead, in the middle of a recession, to sell the world's most expensive hamburger. Boulud, arguably New York City's most famous French chef, had in 2001 introduced the DB Burger, a twenty-nine-dollar foie-gras and short rib–stuffed meatball, as a lark at his new Times Square restaurant, DB Bistro Moderne. Though intended more or less as a joke, the burger quickly became the restaurant's signature dish—the culinary equivalent of bringing a sitcom character in for comic relief and having the show turn into a platform for his catchphrases. Boulud had to like the business the burger brought his sleekly brilliant restaurant, which was in the position of having to compete for Times Square tourist and theater traffic with places owned by quarterbacks. But he never saw it coming and shrugged off his success as good fortune. The ancient and primitive Old Homestead Steakhouse, though, saw a market. Equally challenged as a red-meat temple in an area populated by skinny fashionistas, the Old Homestead regarded Boulud's success with envious eyes. So it came up with a mammoth twenty-ounce Kobe burger. The forty-one-dollar Kobe burger was even more unwieldy than the DB burger, but it brought in just as many customers. Boulud fought back with a fifty-dollar DB Royale, which featured three separate layers of shaved Périgord truffles. These dishes could be considered an anomaly but for the way they were immediately, and successfully, emulated by a dozen other New York restaurants.

The "gourmet burger" phenomenon was duly noted in every one of the many centennial celebrations of the hamburger that appeared in 2004, commemorating the fictional invention of the hamburger at the Saint Louis World's Fair. It seemed a perfect cap to the story and needed no exaggeration. The burger was still going strong, conquering new worlds. Manhattan grandees were paying fifty bucks for hamburgers at the city's best restaurants; McDonald's was reckoned among the largest corporate landowners in Russia.[11] Hipsters in Red Hook, Brooklyn, flocked to a stylized burger restaurant, Schnäck, which featured an earring-wearing hipster as its mascot.

It was at the movies, however, that the hamburger showed its symbolic power most forcefully. In 2003, *Raising Victor Vargas*, a much-lauded film about the lives of contemporary Dominican tenement dwellers on New York's Lower East Side, was released. The film starred real-life *Loisaidas* and was praised for its realism. Its climax involved the young hero inviting his new girlfriend to the family's apartment for a hamburger dinner. Director Peter Sollett remembers, "When we were doing press for the movie, in Paris, and at Cannes, a journalist asked if we were trying to make a point about the way immigrants are stripped of their culture when they come to the United States, by the fact that they were eating hamburgers and not Dominican food. And the answer is,

Every period in American culture has to accommodate the burger.
Brooklyn's Schnäck sought to put it in the context of late 1990s
hipsterism with its mascot, Zack Schnack, and succeeded.

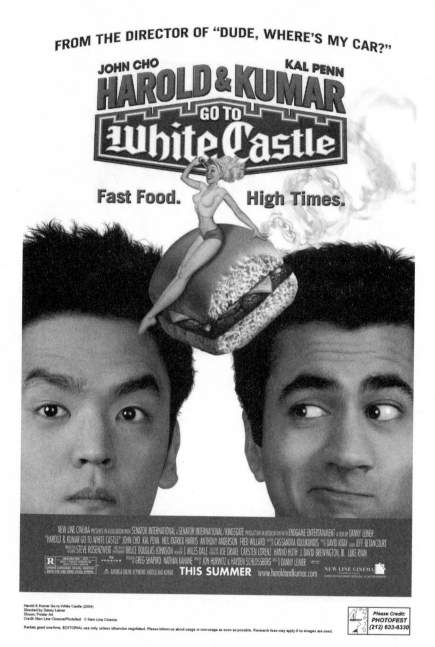

A new generation of American immigrants knew to go to the source
for their hamburger needs.

absolutely not. In Victor's real life family, all the kids' favorite food are hamburgers."[12] In 2004, in time for the hamburger's centennial, the documentary *Hamburger America* was released, celebrating the hamburger. Filmmaker George Motz limited himself to featuring restaurants that had been serving primarily hamburgers for forty years or more and that reflected unique local traditions. Presented without voiceover narration, the film ranges from Memphis to New Mexico to Chicago, lovingly recording local burger ways as an expression of America. And in a coincidence of special poignancy, a teen comedy was released the same year. In *Harold and Kumar Go to White Castle*, two Asian-American college students get stoned and encounter a gamut of white stereotypes on their pilgrimage to White Castle. Film critic A. O. Scott, in the *New York Times*, wrote that the two "could be poster children for early 21st-century American diversity . . . except that the very word would totally kill their buzz."[13] There was some symmetry to this. It was, after all, White Castle that created the hamburger from the fabric of immigrant experience and helped make it an American icon; fitting, then, that it should come around again to welcome another group of immigrants into the fold. America was infinite, absorptive, an idea that transcended physical shape and borders. The hamburger, its most universal symbol, could be no less immortal.

Notes

ONE

The Hamburg-American Line

1. Hannah Glasse, *The Art of Cookery, Made Plain and Easy,* 7th ed. (London, 1763), 370.
2. E. Wade received Patent Number x5348 on January 26, 1829, for what may be the first patented meat cutter. The patent shows choppers moving up and down onto a rotating block. G. A. Coffman of Virginia received Patent Number 3935 on February 28, 1845, for an "improvement in machines for cutting sausage-meat" using a spiral feeder and rotating knives something like a modern food grinder.
3. Fannie Farmer, *The Boston Cooking-School Cook Book* (Boston: Little, Brown, 1896), 178.
4. In 1802, the *Oxford English Dictionary* defined Hamburg steak as a "hard slab of salted minced beef, often slightly smoked, mixed with onions and breadcrumbs. The emphasis was more on durability than taste."
5. Eric B. Ross, "Patterns of Diet and Forces of Production: An Economic and Ecological History of the Ascendancy of Beef in the United States Diet," in Ross, ed., *Beyond the Myths of Culture: Essays in Cultural Materialism* (New York: Academic Press, 1980).

6. Richard Osborn Cummings, *The American and His Food: A History of Food Habits in the United States* (Chicago: University of Chicago Press, 1940), 16.

7. See Mary Yeager Kujovich, "The Refrigerator Car and the Growth of the American Dressed Beef Industry," *Business History Review* 44, no. 4 (1970): 460–482.

8. See, e.g., Ben Rogers, *Beef and Liberty: Roast Beef, John Bull and the English Nation* (London: Vintage, 2004).

9. Austin Flint, Jr., M.D., *The Physiology of Man* (New York: D. Appleton, 1866), 70.

10. Richard Henry Dana, *Two Years before the Mast: A Personal Narrative of Life at Sea* (New York: Modern Library, 2001), 285.

11. Elisabeth Rozin, *The Primal Cheeseburger: A Generous Helping of Food History Served on a Bun* (New York: Penguin, 1994), 37.

12. Robert H. Wiebe, *The Search for Order* (New York: Hill and Wang, 1967).

13. Frank X. Tolbert, *Tolbert's Texas* (Garden City, NY: Doubleday, 1983), 130–136.

14. "Tamales Calientes: Push-Cart Purveyors Who Flourish at Night," *Los Angeles Times*, Sept. 23, 1894.

15. Weber's Web site: http://www.webersoftulsa.com/webers_story.asp.

TWO

"All This from a Five-Cent Hamburger!"

1. Quoted in David Gerard Hogan, *Selling 'Em by the Sack: White Castle and the Creation of American Food* (New York: New York University Press, 1997), 131.

2. Bruce Barton, *The Man Nobody Knows* (Indianapolis, IN: Bobbs-Merrill, 1925).

3. Barton, *The Man Nobody Knows*, 18–19.

4. James B. Twichell, *Adcult USA: The Triumph of Advertising in American Culture* (New York: Columbia University Press, 1996), 6.

5. Ronald L. McDonald, *The Complete Hamburger: The History of America's Favorite Sandwich* (Secaucus, NJ: Carol, 1997), 14.

6. Quoted in Hogan, *Selling 'Em by the Sack*, 26.

7. E. W. Ingram, *All This from a Five-cent Hamburger! The Story of the White Castle System* (New York: Newcomen Society in North America, 1964), 12.

8. Quoted in Jeffrey Tennyson, *Hamburger Heaven* (New York: Hyperion, 1993), 24.

9. Ingram, "All This from a Five-Cent Hamburger!" 9.

10. Quoted in Philip Langdon, *Orange Roofs, Golden Arches: The Architecture of American Chain Restaurants* (New York: Knopf, 1986), 30.

11. *White Castle House Organ*, Aug. 13, 1927, 1.

12. Robert H. Wiebe, *The Search for Order* (New York: Hill and Wang, 1967).

13. Quoted in Daniel Boorstin, *Americans: The Democratic Experience* (New York: Random House, 1973), 114.

14. Quoted in Boorstin, *Americans*, 322.

15. Ingram, *All This from a Five-cent Hamburger*, 22.

16. Ingram, *All This from a Five-cent Hamburger*, 22.

17. John A. Jakle and Keith A. Sculle, *Fast Food: Roadside Restaurants in the Automobile Age* (Baltimore: Johns Hopkins University Press, 1999), 113.

18. The belated adoption of cheese to hamburgers is one of the great mysteries of American food history. It was invented early on, between 1924 and 1926, by an inspired grillman named Lionel Sternberger at the Rite Spot diner in Pasadena, California. But despite the manifest genius of the design, for some reason cheeseburgers remained a regional style for many years. White Castle and its imitators did not adopt cheese until many years later.

19. *Time*, Jan. 11, 1943.

THREE
The Organization Man

1. Ronald L. McDonald, *The Complete Hamburger: The History of America's Favorite Sandwich* (Secaucus, NJ: Carol, 1997), 35.

2. Quoted in David Halbertstam, *The Fifties* (New York: Villard, 1993), 157.

3. Quoted in John F. Love, *McDonald's: Behind the Arches* (Toronto: Bantam, 1986), 14.

4. McDonald, *Complete Hamburger*, 37.

5. Halberstam, *The Fifties*, 159.

6. Ray Kroc, with Robert Anderson, *Grinding It Out: The Making of McDonald's* (Chicago: Henry Regnery, 1977), 7, 8.

7. Kroc, *Grinding It Out*, 8.

8. Kroc, *Grinding It Out*, 9.

9. Quoted in Halberstam, *The Fifties*, 70.
10. Quoted in Halberstam, *The Fifties*, 70.
11. Love, *McDonald's*, 91–92.
12. Love, *McDonald's*, 144.
13. Ted C. Hinckley and Roderick C. Johnson, "Ray Kroc, Embodiment of Mid-Twentieth Century America," *Journal of the West*, January 1986, 94–102.
14. John Higham, "The Cult of the 'American Consensus,'" *Commentary*, February 1959, 93–100.
15. William Whyte, *The Organization Man* (New York: Simon and Schuster, 1956), iii.
16. Kroc, *Grinding It Out*, 103, 109.
17. *Time*, "Franchising: New Power for 500,000 Small Businessmen," Feb. 18, 1969, 43.
18. Quoted in Philip Langdon, *Orange Roofs, Golden Arches: The Architecture of American Chain Restaurants* (New York: Knopf, 1986), 82.
19. Quoted in Halberstam, *The Fifties*, 165.
20. Quoted in Kenneth I. Helphand, "The Landscape of McDonald's," *Journal of American Culture* 1, no. 2 (1978): 357–362, italics added.
21. Love, *McDonald's*, 158.
22. Quoted in Love, *McDonald's*, 156–157.

FOUR

Have It Your Way

1. Elisabeth Rozin, *The Primal Cheeseburger: A Generous Helping of Food History Served on a Bun* (New York: Penguin, 1994), 57, 61.
2. Thomas Hine, *Populuxe* (New York: MJF, 1999), 12.
3. Hine, *Populuxe*, 6.
4. Tom Wolfe, *The Electric Kool-Aid Acid Test* (New York: Farrar, Straus and Giroux, 1968), 48.
5. Langdon, *Orange Roofs, Golden Arches: The Architecture of American Chain Restaurants* (New York: Knopf, 1986), 84.
6. Jeremy Rifkin, *Beyond Beef: The Rise and Fall of the Cattle Culture* (New York: Dutton, 1992), 127.
7. John F. Love, *McDonald's: Behind the Arches* (Toronto: Bantam, 1986), 129.
8. "Man the Barbecuer," *New York Times*, Sept. 16, 1950, 13.
9. David Potter, *People of Plenty: Economic Abundance and the American Character* (Chicago: University of Chicago Press, 1958).

10. A. J. Liebling has chronicled this episode, and the media's handling of it, in an especially vivid and hilarious essay called "The Great Gouamba." *Gouamba* is an African word meaning "meat lust," which Liebling remembered from the adventure books of his youth. A. J. Liebling, "The Great Gouamba," in Liebling, *The Press* (New York: Pantheon, 1975), 139–147.

11. "Hamburgers for Persia: Life and Needs in Iran Described," *Los Angeles Times*, Jan. 21, 1952; "Beef Eating at an All-Time High in U.S.," *Los Angeles Times*, Sept. 2, 1956, 25.

12. James McLamore, *The Burger King: Jim McLamore and the Building of an Empire* (New York: McGraw-Hill, 1998), 45.

13. McLamore, *Burger King*, 45.

14. Kroc, *Grinding It Out*, 134.

15. Robert Hughes, "Roll Right Up, Folks," *Guardian*, Mar. 7, 2005.

16. *The Whole Earth Catalog* (Menlo Park, CA: Portolo Institute, 1968), 43.

17. Susan Sontag, "Notes on 'Camp,'" in Sontag, *Against Interpretation, and Other Essays* (New York: Farrar, Straus and Giroux, 1966), 280.

18. "Pop Art: Cult of the Commonplace," *Time*, May 3, 1963.

19. "Pop Art."

20. Quoted in David Gerard Hogan, *Selling 'Em by the Sack: White Castle and the Creation of American Food* (New York: New York University Press, 1997), 165.

21. "The Burger That Conquered the Country," *Time*, Sept. 17, 1973.

FIVE
The Hamburger in Power

1. Roger Ebert, "Review of 'American Graffiti,'" *Chicago Sun-Times*, Aug. 11, 1973, available at http://rogerebert.suntimes.com/apps/pbcs.dll/article?AID=/19730811/REVIEWS/301010301.

2. See, for further examples, "The 50s in the 1970s: Representations in a Cultural Revival," in Daniel Marcus, *Happy Days and Wonder Years: The Fifties and the Sixties in Contemporary Cultural Politics* (New Brunswick, NJ: Rutgers University Press, 2004).

3. John F. Love, *McDonald's: Behind the Arches* (Toronto: Bantam, 1986), 473.

4. Joan Lang, "The Ethnic Food Explosion," *Restaurant Business*, July 1, 1986, 142–143.

5. Eric Schlosser, *Fast Food Nation: The Dark Side of the All-American Meal* (New York: Houghton Mifflin, 2001), 197.

6. Jeremy Rifkin, *Beyond Beef: The Rise and Fall of the Cattle Culture* (New York: Dutton, 1992), 1–2.

7. Eric B. Ross, "Patterns of Diet and Forces of Production: An Economic and Ecological History of the Ascendancy of Beef in the United States Diet," in Ross, ed., *Beyond the Myths of Culture: Essays in Cultural Materialism* (New York: Academic Press, 1980), 214.

8. Marvin Harris, "How Beef Became King," *Psychology Today* 12, no. 5 (1978): 34.

9. Schlosser, *Fast Food Nation*, 197.

10. "When a Brand Becomes a Stand-In for a Nation," *New York Times*, Mar. 30, 2003.

11. Erin Arvedlund, "McDonald's Becoming Largest Corporate Land Owner in Russia," *Agribusiness Examiner*, Mar. 22, 2005.

12. Interview with Peter Sollett, August 27, 2006.

13. A. O. Scott, "'Harold and Kumar': A Dumb Stoner Comedy for a New American Century" *New York Times*, July 25, 2004.

Illustration Credits

Index

Page numbers in italics indicate illustrations